EMOTIONAL

RESONANCE

First Sentient Publications edition 2005

Cover design by Kim Johansen
Book design by Timm Bryson

Library of Congress Cataloging-in-Publication Data

Watkins, John G. (John Goodrich), 1913-
  Emotional resonance : the story of world-acclaimed psy-
chotherapist Helen
Watkins / John G. Watkins.-- 1st Sentient Publications ed.
      p. cm.
  Includes bibliographical references.
  ISBN 1-59181-042-6
  1. Watkins, Helen Huth. 2. Psychotherapists--Biography.
3. Ego
(Psychology) I. Title.

RC438.6.W38W38 2005
616.89'14'092--dc22

2005022201

Printed in the United States of America

10 9 8 7 6 5 4 3 2 1

SENTIENT PUBLICATIONS, LLC
1113 Spruce Street
Boulder, CO 80302
www.sentientpublications.com

EMOTIONAL RESONANCE

*The Story of World-Acclaimed
Psychotherapist Helen Watkins*

John G. Watkins, PhD

SENTIENT PUBLICATIONS

CONTENTS

FOREWORD

Nothing will prepare the reader for the emotions of the following pages. Those who know the end of the story will know that Helen Watkins died of a massive stroke. Her husband, Jack Watkins, is resolving his grief by sharing her personhood with all of us who knew them both and with those who will follow.

By doing so, he tells us what matters is that we must be real inside, not just well-informed about our scientific work, but genuine at the center of our being, where the art of therapy, that mystical fusion of discipline and intuition, takes root and thrives.

We are privileged to be invited into their home and into their lives: past, present, and uncertain future. No holds are barred. In the final moments, his loss is unimaginable.

Jack and Helen had both been married twice before. They were both in the second half of their lives. Both had children and professional responsibilities. She was born in Bavaria and raised by a beloved grandfather. Jack had a more Spartan upbringing, with a father and mother who didn't teach him the tenderness of love. He was the professional scholar with enormous academic strengths; she was the established psychotherapist equipped with a powerful instinct for healing and health.

This commemoration of Helen's life is the story of a courageous woman who loved and was loved by all who knew her. She had many sides to her personality and great flexibility in taking into herself the hopes and pains of all who knew her: patients, colleagues, and her husband.

She was devoted to the traditions of her childhood, baking cookies from Thanksgiving to Christmas for gifts to family, friends, and the staff at the University of Montana Counseling Center. She had no choice. It was as if she followed an invisible drive to celebrate her origins in this special way.

The stories told about her in this beautiful book reveal a woman who was deep, playful, laughing, and who felt her patients' grief and distress in her own special way, so that they might find more freedom to live well and honestly. She was centered, authentic, and she was in love with Jack.

Jack brought structure to Helen's professional life. He was her bedrock of reason and science. However, that was not enough. She needed a loving partner.

As the years pass, Helen will be remembered as one of the most influential woman therapists our generation has known. Her seminal work with Jack on Ego-State Therapy will stand as a beacon to therapists for succeeding generations. She will be a major model for women and men on their journey to finding their own voices, and in practicing the art of therapy.

—Peter B. Bloom, M.D.
Clinical Professor of Psychiatry,
University of Pennsylvania School of Medicine

Helen Watkins at age twenty-one.

PREFACE

This is the story of Helen Huth Watkins, born Helyanthe Maria Wagner in Bavaria. World acclaimed and loved as a creative therapeutic genius, she drew to herself many psychiatrists, psychologists, and other health workers from the United States and other nations for their own personal therapy.

This book has been written at the request of many of her students, clients/patients, colleagues, and associates who asked to know more about her as a human person, how she lived outside the professional setting.

Endowed with a therapeutic self, she left all whom she touched happier and better off, and her life was spent dispensing gifts to others: the gift of respect, the gift of laughter, the gift of tears, the gift of understanding—and the gift of healing and love.

It is also a love story written by one who was privileged to share thirty years with her as husband, best friend, constant companion, colleague, coauthor and sweetheart—one who himself needs to write this book as a tribute to her, and to relieve the pain of saying good-bye.

Together we journeyed through many countries, sharing our understanding of human nature and ways of treating personal problems with colleagues in universities, medical schools, and scientific societies—she through her constant humanity, wit, and personal demonstrations, I with more academic rationales.

Many basked in her sunshine, perhaps only an hour a week, or a twelve-hour weekend in her professional consulting office. But so many others were touched by her presence simply through casual remarks while waiting on our table at a restaurant, or sitting next to her during an airplane trip.

This is a story about her personhood, her essence, not her therapeutic techniques, which are described elsewhere.[1] It is also a glimpse into what it is like to be a psychotherapist and to be married to one.

Perhaps this book will help continue her legacy of binding the emotional wounds of others. Why must her unique, creative manner of caring cease because she has physically departed? Might it continue longer? She would like that.

—JGW

Helen Watkins, Clinical Psychologist.

THE COOKIE LADY

In a far corner of the basement at our sixty-year-old house, there is an old-fashioned pantry. When you open the door you see a stack of shelves on both sides of it and on the back. In earlier times, when Helen lived there with her young children, those shelves each fall would be lined with glass quart jars filled with peaches, pears, cherries, and green beans, plus jars of jam and jellies.

Today, as in many years, there is a stack of plastic buckets, piled on top of one another—twenty, maybe thirty. They are eight to ten inches in diameter; colored red, blue, and green; and decorated with pictures of fir trees, holly, Santa Clauses, and children playing.

Immediately after Thanksgiving, Helen would begin the annual ritual of making the cookies. This would take all her spare time, evenings and weekends. I would sometimes participate, often resenting the amount of time involved. It took her away from other activities in which I wanted her company.

She would mix dough, flatten it, pound it, cut it into different shapes, bake it, and fill the buckets with *springerle*, *pfeffernusse*, Viennese fingers (yummy chocolate tips), French creme wafers, many kinds of *lebkuchen* and *hasselnussen* (hazelnuts). Those damn *hasselnussen!* She needed my help most with them. Every single small nut had to have the tough, dark brown husk scraped off with a knife. "If you don't, they will taste bitter," averred Helen.

There was something obsessive about this Christmas ritual of the cookie making. I never quite understood it. But if she wanted it, then I would help her.

Why did she do it? My first reaction to her cookie making was that it was simply a compulsion—she did it because she had always done it. Her mother and grandmother had done it. She had to do it. It was instinctual—like the birds flying south in the winter and the Montana bears holing up in their dens.

But to her it was like a religious ritual. Many people go to church on Christmas. They profess their love for Jesus and are reassured that Jesus loves them in return. To Helen, the baking of cookies had a unique, Christmas, spiritual meaning. I never understood it until her daughter, Karen, enlightened me as to its real meaning.

"Did you know that her mother was a gourmet cook and taught her how to make all these cookies? When she bakes them every Christmas she identifies with her mother—really becomes her own mother at that time. She resonates with her mother.

As a therapist, of course, I knew the meaning of *resonance*, but I hadn't realized the extent to which Helen's ability in this area permeated her life so early in her career. I knew that Anna Marie, Helen's mother, was a gourmet cook and had taught her skills to Helen. I just hadn't put it all together. Now I understood. During those moments Helen departed from her usual self and joined the cookie-making state of her loved mother. She was, for the time, her own loving *Mutter* making cookies for her own child self—and she was happy. For the students whom she treated, her cookies were her gifts of compassion and understanding.

The more I thought about it, the more I realized that this ability to resonate lay at the heart of Helen's unique ability to be therapeutic with others. She understood others because she could feel their needs within herself. She sharpened this resonating ability during her years of treating students at the university's counseling center.

❧

Today, I had helped her bring the stack of buckets filled with goodies to the center. They were doled out—big ones for Jim, Fred, Carl and Bill, her close professional colleagues, and also for Berta and Pauline, who typed her clinical reports. Then there were somewhat smaller ones for the graduate assistants. Everybody was happily preparing to go home for the Christmas vacation—and Helen just glowed.

It was Friday, exactly 5:00 PM. The buzzer sounded through the college halls, signaling the end of the last period. Those few students who had not left early, but had conscientiously remained for their final classes, rushed out from the dorms and fraternity houses, and packed their cars or headed to the airport. They would go home and receive well-deserved rewards from family and Santa Claus.

This academic quarter had been a heavy one. Just before Christmas was a time when many college kids got depressed, those that dreaded the days when everybody else was making merry. Helen had been treating a number of such students. Judy and Henry were among them.

Judy was a skinny, dark-haired freshman from a northern Montana ranch. This was her first time away from home, and she was scared. There were so many students at the university, not like her rural high school. And Missoula, with its thirty-five thousand inhabitants, posed a bewildering challenge for an eighteen-year-old farm girl. She and Helen had been talking about these problems.

Outside, bitter cold laid siege to the university. It had snowed the night before, and now the temperature was ten below zero. A blizzard-like wind roared down the Rattlesnake Canyon, making even the college buildings seem to shiver. Judy and Helen put on their heavy winter coats, and Helen pulled on her new brown fur gloves, while admiring them.

She had told me she would like new gloves for Christmas, but when the weather turned frigid, she decided they were needed at once. I told her to go to the mercantile and buy what she wanted, and I would pay for them.

Helen and Judy walked slowly down the counseling center's icy steps, hanging on to the railing and bracing themselves against the wind. Judy had one more thing to say. "I don't want to go home, Helen. Mom will just bawl me out and say I'm not trying hard enough—because I got a B in Econ. If I don't get all A's she tells me how hard she and Dad are working to send me to college, and that I ought to be grateful."

Helen thought silently, *How many parents expect perfection in their children—probably to make up for their own insecurities?* She put her arm around Judy. "Well, it'll only be two weeks."

Judy continued: "I sure wish you were with me—back in Cut Bank. If I had your strength I could stand up for myself, not have to put up with her nagging."

Helen thought a minute. Then, reaching down decisively, she pulled off one of her new gloves. "Here, take this! Put it in your pocket. Anytime you need some strength, hold onto it and imagine I am there right beside you." Judy took the glove, questioningly but gratefully.

When she returned to school in January, she reported a successful and happy holiday season. She had not allowed herself to be dominated by her mother—and Mother even respected her more. Another step in growing up. By spontaneously resonating with Judy's need, Helen gave her the simple support required.

For several weeks now Helen had been struggling with Henry, a young Vietnam veteran was obsessed with killing himself.

"Every time I see a knife I think, 'Do it now! Do it now!' Then, when I'm driving the car down the canyon to school, I think again, 'Do it now! Do it now.' I have to hang on tight to the wheel to keep from spinning it and dashing the car and me down into the river. I don't think I can hold out much longer." He would then burst into sobbing—and he was a tough, battle-hardened veteran back from Vietnam.

After two months in a veterans' hospital, he was discharged. The psychiatrist at the student health service had told him he wouldn't really kill himself and gave him some pills. Helen wasn't so sure. She decided on a more drastic tactic.

"Henry, just lean back in the chair and close your eyes. You are going into a deep, very deep relaxation. I want you to see yourself at the top of some stairs. You and I together are going to walk down those stairs. I will count steps, and with each count we will go down one step more. You can slide your hand along the banister. One—two—three—four—five—six—seven—eight—nine—ten. Deeper, deeper, deeper." He gradually relaxed, and after ten minutes seemed to be in a profound hypnotic state.

"Now Henry, we are at the bottom of the stairs. You can see a hallway, and there are rooms on each side of it. Walk down the hall and stop when you come to one special room."

"Oh, you've stopped at one. What does the door look like?"

"It's large, brown and has a big knob."

"Open that door and go in!"

Henry frowned, "I don't know. It's very hard to open. I don't think I can open it."

Helen thought, *Resistance.* She said, "Maybe if I stood right beside you—perhaps I could help you open it."

After a little struggle, Henry reported, "I think it's opening now."

"Go in and see what you find," Helen instructed. "What's inside that room?"

Henry stiffened! He looked very startled. Then he whispered, "Jesus Christ."

Although she had used this technique before, she was surprised. "Did you say, Jesus Christ? Is Jesus in there?"—as she sub-verbally uttered a "Jesus Christ" (but with a different connotation). "What's he doing there?"

"I don't know," replied Henry.

"Ask Him!" prompted Helen.

He looked very puzzled. "Jesus says, 'You have desecrated my house, and you haven't paid the price.'" Henry shook himself, and immediately emerged out of hypnosis. "I think I know what that means."

"Tell me!" urged Helen.

"When I came back from Nam, I was mad at the world, mad at God, felt anxious, couldn't sleep. So one night I went to the church and set a fire in it. There wasn't much damage. The firemen came and put it right out. But there were a lot of things burned inside."

Helen remembered reading about the incident in *The Missoulian*. A Vietnam veteran had returned in an anxiety state and had set fire to the local church. He had been charged and brought before a justice of the peace. However, since it was recognized that he was very disturbed as a result of the war, and since he had never been in any trouble with the law before, the charges were dismissed, and nothing ever came of it.

Helen thought, *He has been unconsciously feeling guilty because he burned the church, and "never paid the price." He must pay the price to get relief from his suicidal compulsion.* "Henry, how much damage was done? Did it cost you anything?

"Maybe three hundred dollars. The insurance paid it."

"How much could you afford to pay a month?"

"Well, with my pension I would have an extra five to ten dollars. After paying board, room, and college expenses, I could spare five dollars a month."

With Helen's help, Henry arranged to send five dollars each month to the church anonymously. The obsession stopped. After that, he ceased feeling a compulsion to kill himself.

When Helen was treating a client, she was completely absorbed with replicating and experiencing within her own self the life problems portrayed by her patient. She focused intensely and became emotionally involved—like most of us do when watching an extremely interesting movie, completely oblivious of other viewers, lights, or ushers.

These were the years when Helen learned to use this resonating to intervene constructively. Later she made it a central technique in more complex hypnoanalytic and ego-state therapies.

Helen felt good about going home that day. Julie could handle her mother, and Henry would not kill himself. Moreover, her cookies had all been baked and delivered. Yes, this would be a happy Christmas.[1]

Jack and Helen at an early workshop, 1979.

THE SECRET OF MIRACLES

It was many Christmases later. Dozing on the living room couch, I was enjoying aromatic smells coming from the kitchen. Then my ears were assaulted: Ring-ring! Ring-ring! Ring-ring! It was annoying. *Why doesn't she get the phone? She's nearer the extension than I am!*

A cheery voice came to me. "Honey, will you take the phone? My hassenpfeffers will burn if I don't get them out of the oven."

Oh yes! The only thing more important than an emergency call from a patient was cookies burning. If that happens, it means I must scrape another batch of hazelnuts.

Ring-ring! Ring-ring! Begrudgingly, I lumbered into her study and picked up the phone, hoping they would hang up before I got there.

"I wish to speak with Helen Watkins," said a very gruff voice.

"It's for you, Dear," I shouted, and into the phone: "Please hold; she'll be right with you."

How was I to know that this case, a very difficult one, would elicit one of her most innovative and creative solutions?

Lifting the phone, Helen heard a very impatient voice: "Helen Watkins? I have been referred to you as an exceptionally outstanding personal therapist."

Helen thought a moment, then asked, "What is your problem? Why are you consulting me?"

The voice replied, "My wife says I am arrogant, and it is absolutely false."

Helen noticed a German accent and asked the man about his life and work, whereupon he revealed to her that he was "the best orthopedic surgeon in the United States" and chief of surgery in a prestigious medical-school hospital. He also reported that under pressure from his wife he had undertaken many hours of personal psychotherapy with highly reputed practitioners but with little effect.

Helen was amazed. She quietly awaited more information, as she wondered why the "best orthopedic surgeon in America" would come to Missoula, Montana, seeking help for his personal problems with an unknown woman therapist, who lacked a doctoral degree.

She recognized that the man talked in a Bavarian accent. Since she then spoke English without any accent, he did not spot her as German. Helen suggested, "I notice you have a German background and probably came from Bavaria."

He was amazed but very impressed. "Yes, I came from Munich. How could you know that?"

Helen replied, "I was born in Augsburg—came to America when I was very young." From then on, the phone call continued with mutual interest.

They exchanged comments relating to Bavaria, its mountains and deep forests, as well as places in Munich (which we had visited), the impressive *Rathaus* (town hall), the two-domed *Frauenkirche* (Church of Our Lady), and the *Hofbrau Haus* (famous beer house). Within fifteen minutes they became friends. In spite of her lack of a doctoral title, he almost immediately liked and trusted her. Maybe it would be safe after all to come for personal therapy to this primitive state, Montana, and not humiliate himself or lower his status.

A week later he arrived. Helen picked him up at his hotel and brought him to our small house, which contained her consulting office. It lay in a middle-class area of modest homes. He obviously perceived its lack of impressiveness but made no deprecating remarks.

During the initial get-acquainted session, Friday evening, she learned that he was born in a wealthy family, whose parents held positions of power in Munich. He described his mother as a "grande dame" who sought prestige and had little compassion for lesser folks. Her son was taught proper manners, instructed in the importance of his family, and held strictly to its customs. Then the doctor informed Helen, "I had a nursemaid who always took care of me when I was very young. If I needed something I would go to her and not bother Mother. Her name was Lonnie. I could always count on her. I guess I loved her very much.

"One day my mother called me to her room and said, 'I think you are getting too dependent on Lonnie, too close to her. That is not good for you. Accordingly, I have discharged her. She is packing her things now.'"

The distinguished doctor hunched down in his chair and looked sad. "I guess I did love her and must have been very hurt when she left me."

But then his strict-upbringing, dutiful-child ego state[1] emerged. He sat upright, and to demonstrate his courage, exclaimed in a strong voice, "Mother was absolutely right. I was getting too close to Lonnie, and it was not good for me."

Helen then knew what needed to be done. She understood his mask of arrogance, his lifelong drive to be recognized as "the best orthopedic surgeon in America," and she decided what she would do in their next session.

She rearranged her office. The comfortable, plush chair was removed; a straight-backed, hardwood chair was put in its place. And, so he could not recline on the couch, a few books were piled on it. She sat on the floor at his feet and they began the session.

I was reading in our living room near her study, paying little attention to sounds until I hear a loud sobbing. I knew immediately what had happened. The little boy ego state within the great doctor had emerged. He had found his Lonnie. The therapy would go well from then on.

During the next two days, many such abreactive sessions were held as he came to release his unconscious anger and understand his childhood. He consciously experienced his inner rage toward the controlling mother and his lifelong drive to live up to her ambitions. He knew why he had to become "the best orthopedic surgeon in America." When he left to return home on Sunday he was smiling.

A week later Helen received a phone call from his wife. "What did you do with him? He seems to be a completely changed man. He is now so pleasant to be around, not at all arrogant."

Helen merely said, "He is better able to understand his childhood."

There was a pause on the other end of the line.

"Could I make an appointment to see you personally for my problems?"

Two weeks later the doctor's wife arrived, already expecting success in her own therapy.

The miracle in this case was not the profound change in his character, but that it occurred in only one weekend. The process of resonance needs further explanation in order to understand her interaction with him in this complex case.

How does one explain miracles? And how does one understand a miracle worker? Helen had been called a therapeutic self, a genius, and a concert artist. Many of her treatments seemed to be miraculous, not merely because they were successful, but because they were accomplished in such a short time, usually within a three-day weekend.

Steckler[2] described Helen as the prodigy therapist, referring to the time near the end of a workshop when she would ask for a volunteer to experience a session of live treatment before a group of thirty to sixty colleagues.

3

It is common in the teaching of professional workshops for leaders to demonstrate their therapeutic techniques, usually by videotape recordings of past sessions, or by a staged demonstration. Few will take an unknown person and administer real therapy cold before a group. The session might turn out to be a failure, resulting in embarrassment to themselves and the volunteer.

However, most of Helen's demonstrations were successful, some even brilliantly so. The volunteer generally experienced the resolution of a specific significant problem. Afterwards, I would explain and critique the session from a theoretical standpoint. The volunteer became the best-understood person in the group, often receiving the admiration and love of the others—who wished that they had had the courage to volunteer.

Nor did Helen doubt her therapeutic ability. Sometimes on a late Sunday, after her weekend patient had left for the airport, I would ask casually, "Well, did you cure her?" And she would just as casually reply (while continuing to stir the cookie mix), "Of course," as if "'how could you doubt it?'"

In my many roles with her—husband, partner, best friend, colleague, and sweetheart—there was one ego state of mine that could be called my scientific one. I was curious. I wanted to know how Helen achieved her miraculous results so often. What went on inside her that brought immediate trust from her patients, and where did she acquire such a skill?

Helen's daughter, Karen, had explained to me that when Helen made cookies she was resonating with her mother. The more I thought about it, the more I realized that this ability to resonate not only lay at the heart of Helen's ability to be so therapeutic with others, but also was the essence of good therapy.

In my book *The Therapeutic Self*[3] I had studied this process intensively. For example: If one had two pianos, held the A key down on one of them, and struck the A key in the other, the first piano would sound A, though in lesser volume. It would resonate with the other. And if one played a Beethoven sonata on the first, the second would, through resonance, play back the same sonata.

Human beings have this ability to resonate with one another. When you are closely attending a movie, where the hero or heroine is in great danger, your own adrenals will be functioning. We can co-experience with another almost every shade of feeling: fear, anger, love, rage, hope, or curiosity. Witness the giving that pours out when suffering and tragedy are portrayed on the screen, such as happened when the tsunami floods struck Asia.

This resonance is the saving grace of mankind. It is what makes us human. Animals apparently can also resonate with their offspring or with loved masters, but the trait is not so common.

And it is the lack of resonating with others that permits some people to be aggressors, thieves, or murderers. During military combat the soldier, when fighting an enemy, must suspend this ability. You can't attack a person with whom you resonate, because you would be harming your own self. You would feel his pain.

It is difficult for a man to resonate with a woman because he hasn't personally experienced her feelings. His own hormones get in the way—Helen called it "testosterone poisoning."

For example, a male therapist is listening to a female patient describe how she had been raped. A normal male response would be to listen eagerly to her story, perceive her as a desirable object, and feel his own sexual motivations rising. However, if he resonates with her (and not the rapist) then he will feel outraged, not sexy.

This is a difficult task for a man's self. He must be so secure in his male identification that he can temporarily permit his underlying feminine component (female ego state) to emerge, and for the moment be executive. If he is not that secure in his masculinity, then he may be afraid that he will become weak or perhaps a homosexual. Males are taught to be a man—"don't cry, don't back down from a fight, be manly." That is why men may not make as good psychotherapists in treating female patients as women clinicians.

When Helen was treating a client, she was completely absorbed with replicating and co-experiencing within her own self the life being portrayed by that patient. She focused intensively, and became personally involved emotionally— like most of us do when we're watching an extremely interesting movie.

She made the other feel: *This is a person I can trust, one who will understand me, who will help me, who will not condemn or harm me, one to whom I can safely share the secrets of my life.*

As a young schoolteacher, I once tore up the exam paper of a cheating student in front of his classmates. That boy did not come to school the next day—or ever again. By my failure to resonate I had destroyed the rest of his education. I still do not feel good about that incident.

When we do not resonate with another, trust does not result. When one individual resonates with another, the second is impelled to resonate back, a counter-resonance. The two mutually trust each other. It was this therapeutic relationship that characterized Helen's treatment cases.

Her unique therapy exemplifies a statement described in my book *The Therapeutic Self.* "It is not what you do to your patient, but how you be with him." An intellectual interpretation, transmitted in words, would not have done the job; it had to be intensely re-experienced within Helen, and then within the patient's own hypnotic regression.

Once the doctor was loved again by his Lonnie, he could relinquish his arrogance and compulsion to prove his worth. He returned to his wife with a structural change in his personality. He need no longer brag. He *knew* he was a loveable, worthwhile person.

During some eleven years I, consumed with scientific curiosity, had attempted to find the secret of the best therapy, and had sought to find the answer in professional literature. I read many books and wrote one,[4] in which I outlined all the systems of psychotherapy I could find. The book annotated one thousand relevant texts.

I never did find *the* best therapy, but Helen demonstrated it to me. She revealed much of her secret when she simply said, "I quit reading psychology books and listened to patients instead" (as did Freud). Since then she followed no manual of techniques but intensely resonated with all her patients. She gave them much more than her immense intellectual knowledge of therapy. She re-experienced (re-lived) within her own self many aspects of every patient, including each of their relevant ego states. This was the secret of Helen's miracles.

One other question remains: Why did the distinguished doctor seek out Helen? Perhaps he knew at some level that he would resist a prestigious male therapist, that he might be reached only by an unknown, simple woman without credentials he could attack, one who would never challenge his need for superiority, one who was not a "grande dame," but more like a servant, nursemaid? Perhaps! The unconscious in each of us often moves in mysterious ways.

Helen and Jack.

Dare the Impossible

In much dismay she came running into my study shouting, "There's a spider on the wall, Jack. Get him!"

Helen was afraid of spiders, buzzing flies, bees, and such; she was not afraid of people, and she dared to enter areas of their lives that were taboo to most psychotherapists.

Therapy is about changing people, usually through words. But Helen carried the helping process into nonverbal levels. If people can communicate and transmit love or rejection to their pets, why can't they do so with humans who have not yet developed verbal language—a skill that came late in the evolution of our species. Helen talked to newborn babies; she talked to fetuses, embryos—and perhaps further.

The validity of memories uncovered under regressed hypnosis has been controversial, with experimentalists arguing that many of the memories are imaginary and not supported by empirical research. I had challenged that view,[1] pointing out that a newborn baby knows the meaning of pain if scalded on her hand, even though she cannot express the experience in words, but can remember verbally later, when she learns to use words. Helen could describe in English playing around the Augsburg castle, although at that time she spoke only German.

Helen believed that many illnesses and maladjustments, such as lifelong depressions, may have started in the womb. They must be treated there. And although the reality of hypnotic regression to such levels is challenged by empirical research, she moved, unplagued by doubts, into what she heard or sensed with her patients.

During her early career at the university counseling center, Helen's clients were primarily college students; later as a psychotherapist in private practice she saw more mature patients, commonly therapists themselves. In both cases she treated more women than men.

For many of those women the problem of abortion was often foremost. Helen had confronted almost every conceivable form of the abortion problem. Although she, herself, never had an abortion, and probably wouldn't have considered one, she was pro-choice in her belief that the welfare of her patient took precedence over that of a fetus or embryo.

In their search for the origins of human unhappiness psychoanalysts seldom explore earlier than the age three. Helen believed that one must look earlier, and she had no hesitation taking her patient into levels where most therapists dared not go—and which most psychologists didn't believe possible. She would often say, "This woman has had three years of psychoanalysis; her problem wasn't solved. They didn't go back far enough. We have to go back to birth."

Helen's ability to resonate with her patient included the entire range of life. She could laugh with a patient in a one-year-old ego state (hypnotically reactivated) and cry with an unborn fetus—even as she could resonate with pets and other animals. Her commitment was for all areas of the patient's life.

But what did she commit? Like any professional she committed her full intellectual (cognitive) attention and knowledge—but much more. Helen committed her entire self, her being, her essence, her personhood, her soul. In the struggle for the patient's welfare she threw in all that was her:

affectively, perceptually, motorically, viscerally, and cognitively—her entire being.

It is almost as if Helen said, "I will follow you everywhere in your existence, not only observing you, but being with you, fusing with you. For this period I will *be* you, and you will *be* me, as together we move through the entire time of your life, back to your origins—and maybe before."

Helen was never afraid that in such depth of resonance she would not return to her own self. She was so permeated with self-confidence and the joy of living, that she had no fear.

When her client was a woman trying to decide about an abortion, Helen's position was neutral. She believed the woman must make this decision herself.

In the first session, the client discussed the facts—data and possible consequences—including her feelings and attitudes. During the second session, these same things were discussed again under hypnosis.

Visualization of the fetus was then suggested, and the patient was urged to speak to it silently, expressing her conflict about the pregnancy. She told the patient to repeat this message at home by closing her eyes and focusing on her abdomen, stroking it gently and asking for a response.

If the patient sensed an agreement from the fetus, Helen had the woman express to the fetus her sorrow, explaining why she could not give it birth—and then experience the fetus as leaving her body. This was often a time for mourning. Sometimes she and her patient cried together.

Helen reported that occasionally the patient miscarried spontaneously before the scheduled operation, and that it resulted in an emotional release. In some cases the dialogue with the fetus brought a sense that it understood and agreed. The patients reacted with a sense of awe, respect, and love for the fetus in its agreement to end its existence. The experience was profound; it left the patient with freedom from guilt.

If no communication came from the fetus, Helen supported any decision the patient made.[2]

Traumas in the Womb

One patient, an art therapist, was making doodles on a note pad, while describing her problem: "I've always had the feeling that I wasn't supposed to live. I've had many years of psychoanalysis, and we worked out some problems, but I never lost that fear."

Helen asked, "What do you know about your birth?"

"Well, my mother said she tried to abort me, but it failed."

Helen responded, "She did it with a coat hanger, didn't she?"

In amazement the patient reacted, "How did you know? The doctor said my shoulder was injured in the attempt."

Helen merely pointed to the note pad. It was covered with doodles shaped like coat hangers.

When hypnotized, the patient moved off the chair onto the floor and scooted herself back into a corner of the room, where she huddled. Helen kept saying, "You're not supposed to die! You're not supposed to die!"

There was a sudden relaxation. The patient emerged from hypnosis. In a follow-up communication, the woman informed Helen that the obsessive fear of dying had disappeared. Helen did not try to explain this recovery theoretically.[3]

In another case (videotaped), a young man seemed stuck in his academic studies. Helen traced it as his seeming to be psychologically stuck when he was born. His mother had told him his birth was very difficult. Under hypnotic regression Helen induced him to re-experience this birth. Helen kept shouting, "You can make it! You can make it!"

He spoke no words but responded by finger signals. He curled up in the fetal position and finally thrust himself out of the chair onto the floor. Had he just completed a psychological birth and gotten closure?

His academically stuck symptom disappeared. Months later, he reported getting good grades for the first time and expressed gratitude to Helen.

꧂

One of our graduate students (Susan) apparently had no "self" and reported she did not recognize exam papers (usually marked A) as having been written by herself. Her world of experience was watching her own actions as happening outside herself, behaviors in which she never participated. Emotionally her pervasive feeling was of having always been rejected.

Helen induced a deep hypnosis and suggested that she go back to where this feeling started. The patient responded as follows (tape recorded):

> Susan: I am alone. My hands are pushing something soft. I feel dread.
> Helen: Of what?
> S: Pressure. Everything. Of existing. Of being born.
> H: How are you going to get away from that pressure?
> S: Be born.
> H: How come?
> S: I have no choice. My arm.
> H: What's happening to your arm?
> S: It's hooked. Feels horrible. Pulled loose. I feel repulsive.
> H: Why?
> S: Because I'm inside her. But there's a part of me that's good. It's the part that will help me live.

The patient had previously reported under hypnosis the existence of an ego state, called "Survivor." Survivor now emerges.

H: Is her destiny to live?
S: I didn't think about her living in the true
   sense of the word. She was already dead, as
   far as real living. She had killed off the self
   inside her already. I couldn't bring that
   back. But I could keep her alive physically.
H: How old do you feel?
S: Very little.
H: Is there any way now that you can energize
   the part that was shut off, and give that
   machine, life?
S: I don't know. It turned off before I came.
H: The part that was shut off, do you know
   what that part was?
S: It was everything that wasn't physical. The
   fear was still there. But all the parts that
   made her a person turned off.

At one time, in an attempt to make Susan feel, Helen
asked me to come to the therapy hour and wrestle with
Susan. The two of us struggled for ten minutes, neither being
able to put the other down. When Helen asked, "What did
you experience?" Susan replied, "I watched two people
wrestling, but I wasn't there."

Helen toiled for two years to revive Susan's sense of self
and give her an "I," but to no avail.

Susan developed a bleeding sore, which did not heal or
recede after surgery. One evening, putting on her best dress,
she went out to the garage, closed the doors, and turned on
the motor of her little car.

This was the only suicide Helen ever had with her
patients. She cried bitterly for one day. Then we never
talked about the case again. Ten years later Helen permitted
me to publish it.

Amy, a professional psychotherapist with a busy practice, consulted Helen for personal therapy after taking workshops with us. She suffered from lifelong episodes of depression and suicide attempts, and she occasionally cut herself and experienced several hospitalizations. She often heard a voice from the Monster, the Angel of Death, an ego state that told her to kill herself.

Between episodes she could function normally within her profession. Ten years of previous therapy had helped, but had not cured the problem.

During two intensive weekends with Helen, she had undergone a fairly traditional ego-state therapy, accessing numerous parts of herself and resolving many conflicts between them. They could be accessed in the Cabin, a safe place in the hypnotic fantasies of the patient. With their help and guidance, she and Helen had explored areas of child abuse and relations with both parents. They were not married when Amy had been conceived.

There was much progress, and Amy wrote a few months after these sessions: "My life has for the most part been wonderful. I enjoyed the energies that were freed up. My creativity was flowing deep and strong."

Unfortunately, her depressive episodes continued. She had to resume antidepressant medication. The therapy was not finished. Something was incomplete. There was a dark monster lurking underneath that impelled Amy to want to kill herself at times.

Under such circumstances, Helen generally felt that the unresolved problem lay deeper, perhaps at birth—or even earlier. She would dare to take her patient into these realms, and she would herself accompany her patient into a resonant co-experience. She would co-suffer and co-fear what was hidden there.

It was in their third, intensive group of weekend sessions when Helen hypnotized her deeply and accompanied her back into the unknown. The patient had made tape recordings of all her treatment sessions. Following is a most significant excerpt.

> Helen: I'm going to ask Joan, your inner advisor, whether it's a good idea to walk into the Shadow [a feared tormentor], or if we should do it by taking her back in time.
>
> Amy: Either way is fine. [Joan emerges and says, "Go back."]
>
> H: I want Joan, Lane, and the Dove [known supportive ego states] to come out—and go back in time with you, Amy. It is as if the days of the calendar are floating away. You are getting younger, and younger, and younger. The leaves of the calendar take you back into your thirties, your twenties, your teens. Slowly but surely you go back to when you were younger. Age 7, 6, 5, 4, 3, 2, 1, 0. And Amy, it will take you back wherever the Shadow was, where it started. Let me know where you are.
>
> There is a long pause. She is silent.
>
> A: A dot.
>
> H: Feel your way around to see where you are. Do you hear anything, do you sense anything?
>
> A: Feel scared.
>
> H: You feel scared.
>
> H: [Wanting to provide more closeness and support to the frightened patient.] "If it's all right with you, I want to put my hand on your shoulder. I'm going with you. You're not alone this time. I know you're scared. We can all face this together. Remember there's Rodney and Joan and Alley and Blaze [other positive ego states], and we can all face this together.

Helen is aware they may be contacting a crucial trauma—confronting the Monster—perhaps a life and death experience. She is mobilizing all Amy's ego-state parts for support. Sometimes, when the patient agreed, Helen asked me to sit in and participate as an auxiliary therapist, especially when an extremely threatening abreaction like this might be impending.

> Jack: I'm here to help, too.
> H: And Jack is here too. And his energy will also help you.
> A: It's dark. It's scary. Tight!
> H: Tight in your chest? Do you have any feelings about how big you are?
> A: A dot.
> H: Like a dot. Really, really tiny.

Helen is seldom amazed by anything new or startling that emerges during therapy. She was this time.

> H: Let's go and be that dot. Something is happening. Maybe some thoughts come to your mind. Maybe some feelings. [A suggestive/projective technique.] You just feel like a little dot.
> A: Accident.
> H: Oh, you're an accident. I see. Now listen to me very carefully, very carefully. I know that somehow you got the impression that you only came to be because you are an accident. That's not really true. You came to be because your father and mother made you. Listen to me! It did not need to happen unless you were meant to be. They must have come together, and you were meant to be because of that energy from whence you came. It's your essence. It's what glows with a white light that produced you.

Amy had visualized a white light often in her dreams and fantasies.

H: Because you were important, because you were meant to be. Because you had a purpose. I don't know what that is, but that you should live. It didn't matter what the parents intended. We can call it mother nature, if you like.

A: I don't believe that.

H: I know you don't. Because here is a little dot, just a little dot.

A: That's the way I feel. I'm afraid! Afraid!

H: That's because you have taken on their feelings. They have nothing to do with you. They came together because they felt some love for each other.

A: But they didn't want me.

H: That may be true. But they felt love for each other. They were the luckiest people in the world that you came to be. You're dealing with people who didn't know what they were doing. And I know that you came before they were married. And they were embarrassed. But they did create you because they loved each other at that time. I want you to think about the energy from whence you came. You were meant to be.

A: [Sighing] The Angel of Death is hollering.

H: Now where does the Angel of Death come from?

A: From God.

H: Right. If God created you, why would he want you to die? Doesn't make sense.

A: Just a little dot.

H: Why would God bother creating you if he didn't want you to be? The Angel of Death

does not come from God. The Angel of
Death comes from what you thought your
parents felt.

A: [Falteringly] They—felt—it was—an acci-
dent.

Helen knows Amy must undergo an abreaction, an emotional release where she experiences all the feelings of her
father and mother, but now understands where they come
from. She can then expunge them from herself, and turn
them into an object, a memory of her parents, no longer a
part of her own self.

H: Now you can feel all their feeling, the
embarrassment, and you can know where it
all came from.

Amy breaks into sobbing as Helen continues her interpretation and *working-through*, as it is called in psychoanalysis.

A: That's all I have. That's all I know.

H: No! That's all you know. What you do
know. You know to send their feelings back.
They're not your feelings. Just let yourself
feel everything you feel, but make sure you
know that these are their feelings.[4]

This complicated, sensitive procedure is like surgical
removal of an internal, psychological cancer, one that Helen
accomplished many times with her innovative techniques.

H: Know the difference. Know what father
feels. Know what mother feels, and know
that these are *their* feelings. They don't
belong to you. When you fully feel that, you
can send those feelings back to them. Now
listen! In a moment I'm going to count to
three, and what I want you to do is to send
their feelings back. Why should you drown
in somebody else's feelings? And we'll get

the feelings that belong to you. One, two,
three. Give it all back! You have no right to
those feelings.

Helen repeats and emphasizes these interpretations
many times. There is some resistance.

H: Now! You told me that God created you.
Now feel that feeling that goes in white
light. He created you. You were meant to be.
You took on all those feelings from mother
and father, and they had nothing to do with
you.

Amy raises the question about hurting herself to get
love. Helen responds, "You don't have to hurt yourself to get
love."

H: Now, I'm going to ask your Inner Advisor,
"Is it a good idea now for her, the little dot,
to grow up and experience whatever she
feels?"
The Inner Advisor ego state emerges and says, "Yes."
A: They're all talking about me. What to do
with me.
J: What are they saying?
A: Mother is saying I'm fine.
J: How does it make you feel?
A: Like I want to cry.

The session ends on a positive note. The lessons here
need more practicing (working through), but a divide has
been crossed. Amy will move toward getting well.

Amy wrote her present-day feelings about her therapy
with Helen:

> Over a three-year period, Helen and I spent
> nine days doing intensive ego-state therapy
> together. She not only saved my life but
> transformed it profoundly. I have experi-
> enced first-hand how another human being
> can therapeutically lend you their energy,
> resonate deeply with your inner processes,
> and guide you in discovering your own inner
> resources. She allowed me to feel safe
> enough to access and face parts of me that
> had remained in the shadows, unexcavated,
> unclaimed and unhealed.

And regarding the dot (which Helen and I did not try to
explain scientifically), Amy wrote: "So many other professionals would have dismissed such a phenomenon. Through
her and your acceptance, this part of my reality, my experience was validated and corroborated. This had a tremen-
dously therapeutic and curative effect."

In this case one can see the long development in Helen
from a counselor who often treated her client with a simple
intervention, like giving a glove or arranging the payoff of a
guilt-provoking debt to symbolically represent her resonance
and loan of self energy. Now she uses the most sophisticated
hypnoanalytic and ego-state procedures, and dares to reach
further back into the unconscious of her patients.

But how did all this professional growth come into a little Bavarian girl, who first came to America speaking only
German? What formed her development into a world-recog-
nized, acclaimed, and loved psychotherapist?

Back row, left to right: Helen's mother, Anna; Helen's sister,
Mary; Grossmutter; Grossvater; Helen's uncle Richard; Front
row, left to right: Helen's uncle Siegfried; little Helen

SUNRISE FOR GROSSVATER

In 1921, throughout Germany, the future looked grim. Depression loomed everywhere. People struggled to survive. In a devastating war the nation had been defeated, suffering over a million casualties. Almost every family had lost fathers and sons. The menfolk had returned with shattered bodies and minds. Families must now care for them, but life savings, which one day could buy a pair of shoes, might not be sufficient the next to purchase a loaf of bread.

Weak governments were helpless, as battles raged between communists, monarchists, and socialists. In Bavaria gangs of hoodlums, led by a rabble-rouser called Hitler, terrorized the honest burghers.

In the 1880s, a strong chancellor, Bismarck, had given the country prosperity and order. The nation then was respected for its scientists, musicians, artists, and writers. However, Kaiser Wilhelm II had dismissed Bismarck and foolishly embroiled his country in a world war.

Wilhelm's mother, an English princess, had suffered a fall from a horse while she was pregnant. Her son was born with a withered left hand, which he blamed on his mother. He never forgave her (or her country) and always hid the left hand in photographs. This disability developed in him a life-long feeling of inferiority.

Perhaps a resulting hatred of women influenced his conviction that they should keep to *Küche, Kirche, und Kinder* (kitchen, church, and children), a position obediently accepted by Helen's warm, nurturing *Grossmutter.*

During the hot July summer of 1921 in the city of Augsburg the pressures on Grossvater, its chief of police, must have been enormous as he tried to enforce the old values of law and order midst the chaos and street battles. Moreover, the family still mourned their eldest son, only sixteen years old, who had been struck down in France on the western front.

Burly and ample around the middle, Grossvater was proof that Grossmutter had fed her family rather well on the meager salary he received enforcing law and order in this city of one hundred thousand souls.

But in that milieu a ray of sunshine was about to enter the chief's life, a tiny granddaughter, born July 19. The child would never see her father, who had died before she was born. Since there was no other means of support, her mother, Anna Marie, had moved back to the parental household.

Anna, who was reading a Greek novel at the time, named the little one, Helyanthe, meaning Flower of the Sun. And indeed the child radiated sunshine constantly into the home of her grandparents. Although they didn't know it, she was destined (as Helen) to bring rays of warmth and healing into the lives of countless others.

Grossvater was immediately conquered by this little bundle of sunshine. He was the stable authority on whom she could always depend and became both father and grandfather to her. She learned early to trust her world—it loved her and would protect her.

Under Hely's sparkle, meaning and laughter returned to the household. And throughout life she had no fear of people in authority. She could challenge any of them, secure in the knowledge that she would never be hurt. As she once told me, "Grossvater said I could do no wrong—and he was right."

She regarded Siegfried and Richard as her brothers, although actually they were her uncles. Toward them,

Grossvater was not so benevolent. Misdoings on their part brought severe punishment, perhaps to be expected from the city's highly regarded chief of police.

This differential treatment of the sexes gave her a childhood view that, "I'm glad I was born a girl, who doesn't have to work or go to war—like men." It was also reflected later in life when she refused to join the Women's Lib movement, proclaiming, "Why should I sacrifice my superiority for mere equality?"

Not that she paraded this view openly, but her belief in the superiority of the female sex was always with her, and women loved her for it. Most of the patients who came to her were women, and the letters of condolence at her death were also mostly from women.

The family stories we have picture her as a rascal, brimming with energy, who enjoyed playing harmless but laughter-provoking tricks on others.

Her young mother, influenced by the flapper generation of the 1920s, prided herself on being modern. This meant that Hely's hair was bobbed, which set her apart from the other schoolgirls. They all wore braids in the old-fashioned tradition. Hely, while laughing, would pull their pigtails, much to their discomfort. Mother would only mildly chide her. And *Grosspapa* would laugh uproariously.

She also enjoyed capturing bugs and putting them down Siegfried's neck—giggling while he chased her. Although he was four years older, he could seldom catch her.

Grossvater had a huge beer stein. It was beautifully engraved with colored pictures of young alpine people dancing and had a hinged silver dome on top. Around the bottom were the words *Bier ist gesund zu jeder Stund* (Beer is healthy all the time).

Grossvater gave her the task of going to the neighboring *Bierstube* and filling his stein with a dark brew. Hely would stop on the way back and take a little slurp. Either he failed to notice that the stein was not completely full, or he overlooked it.

As a grown-up, Helen never became an alcoholic, but whenever we visited Munich on our professional travels she would get into a laughing jag over beer and wurst at the Hofbrau Haus. I often wondered how the flaxen-haired waitresses, who were built like army tanks, could carry six mugs on each arm.

❧

One time Hely attracted much attention by confronting authority in school. Most Bavarians were Catholic. The public schools there were Catholic and taught by nuns. Apparently this particular day the teacher had stated that, "All Protestants will go to hell."

Infuriated, little Hely rose to her feet. "That's not true," she shouted. "You are lying. I have friends who are Protestants, and they're not going to hell."

The entire class was aghast. Little schoolgirls did not challenge teachers, let alone nuns (who were backed by the authority of God himself). There was a great commotion in the class. How could she dare?

The teacher sternly quieted the disturbance, and Hely was banished to the corner. She stood there looking out the window, philosophizing on life. The great tower on the canal, like Grossvater, stood as a pillar of strength with which she could identify.

When she came home that day Grosspapa only chuckled and said, "Maybe it isn't a good idea to confront your teachers in front of the other students." She felt righteous and secure. For Helyanthe, the real authority had stood firmly behind her.

Grossvater was her role model. He must have been the kind of police officer who communities seek, one who is incorruptible and manifests the highest integrity. From him, Helen acquired a strong ethical sense of right and wrong. She also perceived him as the dispenser of justice. He could apprehend wrongdoers and put them in jail. And even though in that age and culture this authority was exercised only by men, Helen, through her identification with him, must have felt that she too had that right.

Grossvater did not administer justice in a cruel or vindictive manner. He was eminently fair-minded, and probably easily overlooked minor infractions. That is why Hely felt it was OK to pull pigtails and put bugs down Siegfried's neck. These were just little jokes and fun. But in my years with her I never saw her act in a vindictive manner and purposely harm another human being.

For Helyanthe, Grossvater was her God. He did what was right. She would be like him and also do what was right. Sometimes this conviction was carried to the point where she perceived that what she did was always right, and that she was justified in doing it. Accordingly, she felt no fear of hell and needed no promise of everlasting life to behave herself. The church, and its forgiveness of sin, had little meaning to her. But little Hely also believed that she, like Grosspapa, had the right to administer justice if she felt unfairly treated.

When her second teeth were replacing the baby teeth, some of them developed askew, especially a tooth that crowded others and protruded, spoiling the evenness of her front uppers. An orthodontist recommended that it be removed and her remaining teeth straightened with braces.

One day her mother was reading in the dentist's waiting room while he was working on Hely. Suddenly a loud scream emanated from his office. Red-faced, he emerged waving a bloody finger and shouting, "Get that girl out of here."

Helen's mother, surmising what had probably happened, gathered their coats, rushed her out the door, and patiently inquired, "What happened, Hely, Did you bite him?"

"Yes! He was a liar. I didn't like him."

"Why didn't you like him?"

"He said it wouldn't hurt, and he didn't tell the truth. It did hurt. I told him so, but he didn't listen to me," Hely replied.

"So?"

"So when he did it again and lied, I bit him." Hely felt quite righteous and vindicated in her action.

Mother didn't know just how to handle this situation, or what admonishments to give. She did nothing. However, they didn't go back to the dentist, and he didn't send a bill. Helen never received further orthodontic treatment. The crooked tooth remained throughout the rest of her life.

She never hesitated to stand up and confront authorities when she felt they were wrong or unjust. Nor did she ever feel in awe of the many distinguished doctors and professors, world renowned in their specialties, whom we came to know as colleagues. And if any of them were surprised at her frankness, laughter soon melted all formality.

❧

Hely often spent afternoons playing by herself in the shadow of the massive walls surrounding Augsburg Castle, peering into the moat, and daydreaming of what the future would bring.

Helyanthe was a romantic. Her imaginative world was filled with fairy tales of knights, princes, heroes, and palaces. When she grew up she would be a beautiful princess. A handsome knight on a white horse would sweep her off her feet and carry her to his castle where they would be married. She would sit on a throne beside him. They would live happily together in their kingdom and have many children.

She knew just what he would be like. He would be young and handsome, a hero in battle—but he would be kind, gentle, strong, and, like Grossvater, completely devoted to her.

She would help all her subjects who were poor or in need and become remembered in history as The Good Queen. Helen never lost these fantasies. They remained hidden unconsciously inside the little Hely.

Grossvater scolded her only one time, and she never forgot it. Hely almost always got top grades in school and was recognized by the teachers as their best student (to the envy of her classmates). And she generally was very honest. But this one time, when she could not answer a test question perfectly, she had glanced at another student's desk and copied the answer down on her slate.

The teacher saw her do this—the same one whom she had challenged about the Protestants. This teacher came to her house and accused her before Grossvater. Hely stubbornly denied the accusation. He was confused. He did not want to believe that his little *Grosstochter* would cheat and lie. But he was the city's representative of law and order. He administered a very severe scolding. Midst tears, Hely continued to deny wrongdoing. But she knew she was guilty, and deep inside her, Grosspapa's reproach hurt very much. Throughout the rest of her life she rarely did wrong, but when she did it was very hard to admit it.

In Germany, Wagners are numerous (like Smiths in America). Hely's family was a well-knit social tribe. During the evenings they would gather together and sing while Richard played the piano. Opera was popular, and Hely had visions of being a prima donna, dying nobly like Carmen, or Violetta in La Traviata.

But now evil threatened Germany. The Nazis, led by Hitler, were mistreating Jews and were poised to take over the government from the revered President von Hindenberg.

Hely and her mother would go to visit Uncle George and Aunt Mary, who lived in America. How exciting! They expected to return to Augsburg shortly, but fate ruled otherwise. The stubborn, independent little *Fraulein* was about to leave Grosspapa's life. He would never see his puckish sunflower again.

What was she like back in Augsburg? Years later, as a birthday present to her, I tried poetically to capture her essence then, as I experienced her in the now.

To Little Hely

Willy nilly poo.
What can he do
When he's got a girl
With blonde hair a-curl
Whose teasing behavior
Gets bolder?
She's muchly alive
And barely aged five
But really believes
She is older.

Her fingers a-wiggle
A poke and a giggle
When he tries to sleep
He cannot go deep
But hopes that drowse
Will enfold her.
'Cause she'll never quit
'Till he gets the wit
To scratch off that itch
On her shoulder.

So willy nilly poo.
What can he do
With a rascally girl
Who's really a pearl,
But keeps him a-twirl
With horns and halos above her?
I guess he must do
What never he'll rue.
Just love her, love her,
And love her.

—Hans

Helen at a costume party on a Caribbean cruise.

HELY AND THE HURRICANE

Anna, Hely's mother, was absorbed in another novel. She liked romantic fiction. The cabin lurched back and forth as the great ship plowed through the high waves. She had difficulty sitting comfortably and concentrating on the book.

A powerful gale howled outside. The North Atlantic often produced a hurricane this time of year. She listened as *Kapitän* Langsdorf warned through the speaker system, "All passengers must stay in their cabins. It is dangerous to walk on the decks this evening. The storm should be gone by morning."

The captain ran a tight ship. In solid Teutonic thoroughness everything was shipshape, the deck chairs pulled back, and the hatches battened down. Anna had thought of going to the dining room for a late snack, but in view of the turbulence and the unsteadiness in walking had decided to forego this trip.

She was a tall woman, with light brown hair, neatly combed, perhaps a bit artificially bleached. But her warm, friendly smile was matched by the bright red silk lounging robe she was wearing. Usually quite relaxed, she was ever available if anything threatened her only child. Her concentration on the interesting novel was frequently interrupted by the ship's motion and would bring a momentary tinge of worry to her placid countenance.

Eleven-year-old Helyanthe lay sprawled on the bed and seemed completely absorbed in *Buch der Lieder* (Book of

Songs) by Heine. Hely deeply enjoyed imaginative, romantic poems and could recite many of them by heart.

During the evenings, when friends and neighbors joined the family back in Augsburg, each one contributed to the entertainment. Hely would recite Goethe's *Heidenröslein* (The Wild Rose). Everybody in the family agreed that the naughty boy who plucked that rose deserved his punishment by the prickly thorns.

She could dramatically throw herself into the story of a father's desperate horseback flight to escape the evil *Erlkönig* (elf king), who sang seductive songs of death. In spite of super-human efforts, the rider finally reached the safety of his farm courtyard. But the child in his arms was dead. Hely and her listeners were in tears by the end of the poem.

Just before Hely and her mother boarded the ship there had been an unpleasant incident. Since the visit to America might be for several weeks, even several months, Grossmutter had packed many changes of clothing into the big green trunk, which was tightly fastened with straps.

Hely had been watching the baggage handler rolling it on a dolly toward the ship. A label attached to the handle informed movers that it was to be sent to Deck D, and transferred to No. 416, their first-class cabin. Grossvater had dug deeply into his savings to provide his loved ones with the finest accommodations. Suddenly, several rough-looking men waving a red flag approached it pointing and shouting. Hely could make out some words like, "Wealthy imperialists," and "Dump this trunk in the water." They had grabbed the trunk and were shoving it toward the edge of the wharf when a larger group of men wearing brown shirts, and with crazy-looking crosses on their sleeves, came running. They chased the first two away.

Hely looked puzzled. "What are all those men doing?" she asked.

Hely could tell by the frown on her mother's face she didn't like what she had just seen. But Anna said only,

"*Macht nichts*" (Not important), and they had then walked up the gangplank.

On board, Hely had been permitted to roam the ship by herself. Anna reasoned, *This is a German ship. There is order, and little girls are quite safe.*

At the library Hely had checked out the Heine book, and another in English. She could not read the English one, but by studying the pictures she got some of its sense. Why did the stupid English print their books in a strange type instead of the correct German script found in her school books? She studied the words carefully and made out a few of the letters. Some day she would read and speak English as well as anybody. Tossing the book aside Hely stretched. She was not yet sleepy, but she was bored.

An unusually large wave hit the Europa, jarring Anna out of an exciting moment when the heroine was in danger of being captured by a villain. She roused and looked about. "Hely. Where are you? Hely. HELY!" Jumping up, Anna looked everywhere.

No! She was not on the bed or in the bathroom. A feeling of dread coursed over Anna. She rushed to the cabin door calling, "Helyanthe. HELYANTHE! Oh! *Mein Gott!* She's run outside."

Forcing the door open, Anna was struck by a wind blast that threw her off her feet. She scrambled up and started running down the deck, dodging sprays of water. *Maybe she's gone down to the lower decks. No, she must have stayed high up.*

Anna kept reassuring herself, *Probably she stayed on this deck.* But one couldn't count on that. Hely was independent and went wherever she pleased.

Anna screamed as loud as she could, "Hely, HELYANTHE!

"Oh, Gott in Himmel! Am I going to lose Hely? Why wasn't I watching her? Grossvater will never forgive me!"

A chubby, red-faced little deckhand appeared. He looked as if he were barely sixteen and reminded Anna of Josef, her older brother who had died on the fields of France.

"Hely's out in the storm," she shouted. "She left when I was reading. She'll get washed overboard. Help!"

The deckhand rushed to her side, "You mean the little Bayerische princess?" he anxiously inquired.

Only four days out of port, Hely knew every hand and servant on her deck by name. The diminutive Bavarian girl had already become a popular celebrity. She had also contacted all the passengers in adjoining cabins. To everyone she had something to say that left them a little happier. Everybody knew the little princess, and everybody was charmed.

But now other cabin doors were opening. Other calls for help rang out. A loose deck chair sailed by, almost knocking Anna off her feet. The little sailor shouted to her, "Go get your raincoat! You'll be drenched!" while he called for more crew.

Anna rushed back into the cabin and grabbed a coat from the closet. When she emerged a few moments later he put his arm around her and, placing his sturdy form so as to protect her from the wind, guided their steps along the slippery deck toward the bow. Occasionally a very high wave would spray over the railings. He would pull Anna back to the inside where they were protected by the overhang of the deck above.

Suddenly Anna saw a dark little figure standing in front of the black and red flag of the German Republic. As waves splashed over it, the little figure would run back into the protection of the front cabin's great window.

Hely was having the time of her life. How exciting it was dodging the spray. Sometimes, she wouldn't anticipate how large a wave was. Then she would get another drenching. It was like the games she and the other children had played in school, throwing bags of water at each other. Hely was nimble and quick, and seldom was wetted. She could run like a boy.

In a panic Anna rushed up to her!

"Hi Mutter. Isn't this fun?"

Furiously angry, Anna screamed! "Helyanthe Maria Wagner. How dare you run away without telling me! You could get washed overboard! Look how dangerous it is, you Dummkopf (blockhead!)"

By this time the two of them had reached the laughing girl. The little sailor wrapped his arms around her soggy dress and started to carry her.

"Put me down. I can walk by mein selbst," she demanded while squirming herself out of his grasp.

"Let her down," said Anna. Then turning toward Hely she demanded, "Hang on to my hand!"

The three of them, bracing themselves against the wind, which was now coming more from the stern, slowly made their way back to the cabin.

"Danke schön," gratefully mumbled Anna.

"Don't worry about the little girl," replied the sailor, smiling. "She'll be all right."

Back in the cabin Anna's breathing returned to normal. Hely, somewhat irked that her fun had been curtailed, resentfully permitted Mother to take off her wet clothes, slip her into a nightgown, and tuck her in bed. She was asleep almost immediately.

Anna, too, was exhausted. She picked up the novel from the floor where it had been thrown and collapsed into the comforting featherbed. *Dank Gott!* She would not have to confront Grosspapa and Grossmutter and describe Hely's being washed overboard during the voyage.

The skies were blue when they awakened the next morning, and the sea was smooth and quiet. Two days later, the great ship moved slowly into New York midst shouting and the tooting of horns. Hely was thrilled, especially watching the Statue of Liberty, about which she had read.

"Mutter, can we stay a long time over here? It must be wonderful to be an American."

Mother only smiled and nodded. Then, as they approached the dock, Hely saw Uncle George and Aunt Mary. She shouted and jumped up and down!

The long voyage was over. As she and her mother made their way through the disembarking passengers, Hely looked back. It had all been so much fun. Approaching the gangplank she spotted the cherub-faced little sailor. He was obviously waiting for her. He held out his hand to give her something. She took it, a little ship model of the Europa that he had carved out of wood. Hely recognized it as a love gift. Throwing her arms around him, she gave him a big hug. Then, skipping briskly down the gangplank, she stopped a moment at the bottom to look back. There he was, smiling and waving at her. She waved back.

꧁꧂

Helen in the early 1980s.

From Little Hely to
Grown-Up Helen

Uncle George and Aunt Mary's house lay within a secluded residential district near Squirrel Hill. It was filled with large, older houses inhabited by the upper middle class of Pittsburgh and surrounded by stately oaks. Hely loved to roam in the forested park a few blocks away and chase the squirrels. They reminded her of Bavaria.

The home was a modest two-story frame building, three bedrooms, fronted with a large porch reached by twenty concrete steps up from the sidewalk. Hely had the small upstairs bedroom, which she decorated with bright-colored pictures. She liked having her own desk; it was piled with many books. She could close and lock her door—which she often did. Having her own private place was important. She could be completely absorbed in a book—Aunt Mary often had to call several times, "Hely, komm essen" (come eat), before she would put it aside and reluctantly traipse downstairs.

When Hely and her mother left Bavaria to visit Uncle George and Aunt Mary in the exciting new land, America, she had been thrilled. They would be gone a month or two. How many interesting things she would have to tell her friends when they returned.

But fate intervened. These were troubled times in Germany. The belligerent Nazis were seizing power. Hely's mother was worried. Uncle George had suggested they stay a little longer until "things quiet down." But things didn't quiet down. Hitler's Nazis took over the government. Socialists, Jews, and others were persecuted. Anna Marie decided to postpone their return.

❧

Today was the first day of school. Hely, all excited and wearing her blue dress, plus her new shiny shoes with white stockings, could hardly wait to get to the big brick building with the spacious playground. It was only a few blocks away. She thought, *These Americans! Just because they have such a wealthy country doesn't mean they are better than Germans.* She would show them. Off she trudged as Mother, Uncle George, and Aunt Mary stood on the porch and waved her well.

Then everything went wrong, very wrong. The first day she came back home, much subdued. Mother wondered why she was so quiet but didn't ask. Maybe school had not met her expectations.

The second day she returned, visibly upset. She would not talk or even respond to Uncle George's patient questioning.

On the third day she exploded! "I don't like school at all. I don't want to be an American. Let's go back to Germany." Hely was angry, just plain mad. It took some time before the family got the story out of her.

She, the center of attention, acclaimed and loved by almost everybody in the past, had encountered a hostile social atmosphere for the first time. "Nobody speaks to me. At recess, those bad boys make fun of me, call me a kraut, and throw stones at me."

Even the principal and teachers hadn't known what to do with this little German girl. She was obviously very intelligent. Her school reports from Augsburg indicated she was always at the top of her class. She had read numerous classics of literature—many more than the pupils in that school. Furthermore, she could handle mathematics like a high school student. But she couldn't speak a word of English.

They compromised. Hely was assigned to the sixth grade. It took a visit from Uncle George to the principal to get the full story. George explained it and then reassured her. "So, it's just because I can't speak English? I'll show them," she vowed. "I'll learn to speak English better than any of them!" She did.

Each day she carefully copied down everything the teacher wrote on the blackboard. She listened to the way everybody talked. Then at home she practiced, trying to mimic their sounds. She watched their every gesture, including the way they moved their lips. She wrote down all the slang expressions she heard and practiced them. She noticed that Americans used their tongue and lips differently from Germans.

"Huh!" commented Hely one day to her mother. "Americans have tight lips. Germans have a lazy way of expressing words. I'll bet it's because they drink so much beer," she laughed.

As she became increasingly proficient in English, her marks in school rose again to the top of her class. Hely determined she would learn to speak just like an American—and without an accent.

At home, George could speak good English—his job as an engineer demanded it. Mary had been in America several years, and Anna was now picking it up. But both of them spoke with a German accent.

❦

More years in Pittsburgh passed. Hely and her mother did not return to Augsburg. Letters were returned. Germany was at war. They heard that Siegfried and Richard were in the German armed forces.

George and Mary had become naturalized citizens—if he had failed to do so he would have been fired from his engineering job. But the nation needed steel and bridges. He was not questioned, especially because he was so competent, and they were regarded as loyal Americans.

Hely, now reconciled to her life in America, would wave the flag and cheer at the patriotic parades. She also cried. Hely always cried at parades, even as at Oktoberfests in Munich, but now the tears stemmed from a secret concern about her brothers, especially Siegfried.

She studied hard, achieved many academic honors, and became a naturalized citizen. She recognized that Helyanthe was an unusual name. It attracted curious attention, but not always favorably. So she changed it to Helen. She was proud to be an American citizen even though she was often beset with a sad longing for her native land.

Helen's natural, spontaneous caring for others made many friends. It was graduation time. There were five thousand students in her high school. However, George, Mary, and her mother were not really surprised when she was selected valedictorian of her class. They had expected it. She could choose to deliver an address or sing a musical selection. Her old longing to be a prima donna won out. She sang an operatic number. But she would never be a diva. A bout with laryngitis shortly afterward removed that possibility. She could still sing, but not with the birdlike voice that had so delighted Grosspapa. Sadly she relinquished her childhood dream. She would go to college and be famous, perhaps become a doctor who could treat people and make them well. She ordered catalogs from Penn State University and made up her mind.

"That's where I can become a great doctor," she announced.

"Liebchen" (Little Darling), said her mother. "I know you really want to go to Penn State, but times are not yet good. Why don't you go here to Pittsburgh University?"

Hely was disappointed. In her mind she had built up her hopes of going to Penn State. She did not like being thwarted, but she was also a realist. She would do what Mother wanted and what she knew George and Mary could afford. Someday she would go to Penn State.

Hely identified with her mother, Anna Marie, who was a very loving person. But Grossvater represented the ideal man. When it came time for her own adult love and marriage, Grandfather would be her model.

What was Grossvater like—as a person? He, first of all, loved his little granddaughter completely. He always supported her. He didn't criticize her. Rarely did he punish her, and then only mildly. He was strong and stable. He was very intelligent. He had integrity. She could trust him completely, count on him. And, as chief of police, he was respected in the community. That is the kind of person she had fantasized for a husband.

But then came Hely's first big loss. Word arrived from Germany that Grossvater had died of a heart attack while working in his garden. Hely was devastated. She had lost the first love of her life. Could she ever find a man who would so completely care for her as Grosspapa?

Helen arriving at a party in Missoula, circa 1990.

Can Fairy Tales Come True?

During high school Helen dated infrequently. Many of the boys appeared to her as superficial, selfish, or lacking in values, sometimes threatening—like those in the sixth grade who had called her "Kraut," and thrown rocks at her. She didn't trust them. She could only love someone who would be like Grossvater.

One boy did earn her trust and eventually her first girl-boy love, Bob. Call it puppy love if you will, but it was genuine, and Hely invested all herself into it.

In her junior year of high school, she had first met this handsome young fellow—courteous, honest, and hardworking. They started dating. She increasingly grew closer to him, and he thought she was the prettiest girl in school. In their senior year of high school they walked to school together every day, he carrying her books. She liked that. He was so unlike all those other crude boys. In her mind he was more like a German. Grossvater would approve of her dating him.

Bob was in the Navy ROTC, and she always thrilled at watching him in uniform when his unit was on parade. They danced together at the junior-senior prom. Anna bought her a beautiful formal dress. And that pink corsage of roses he brought her just matched it.

Helen, herself, told me that Bob reminded her of Grossvater. He shared the same values and behaved in similar ways. He could be trusted—unlike other boyfriends.

Helen would marry him. They would live on naval bases, and she would become a navy wife. It could be a happy existence, with a respected husband. They would have children, and (perhaps) in time she would find a career for herself.

If she stayed at home, and went to school in her home town, she would not be separated from Bob. This clinched her decision. She could attend the University of Pittsburgh and continue seeing him.

Events abroad began to influence plans in America. Hitler's armies invaded and conquered first German Sudetenland and then Austria. War broke out, and finally in 1941 involved this country.

When war came to America, Bob was called up and sent to various bases for training as a combat pilot. Helen lost her zest for college and felt it would be patriotic to seek a war-related job. She got a position in the military New York office of an Air Force unit developing psychological tests.

Strangely, the director of that unit was a man who had been my boss at the Alabama State Personnel Department, where I had spent my summers improving tests for state personnel. Helen's and my paths passed near each other then—but did not cross. Anyway, it would not have been the right time for Helen and Jack.

⁂

A letter came from Bob to Helen. Soon he would be sent to the San Diego Naval Base preparatory to being shipped to the South Pacific. They decided to marry without delay. She traveled to Jacksonville, Florida. Their military wedding (crossed swords) was held in a little church. Bob's orders came through, and the happy couple left for San Diego.

Helen was in love, intensely in love. She was now the beloved wife of her strong, handsome hero, he with an integrity like that of Grossvater. All of Helyanthe's romantic dreams from childhood had come to pass. Like the knight on the white horse, her prince had transported her to their new home—even if only a naval base in San Diego—not a great castle. That would come in time.

His orders stationed him on a carrier that was headed for the South Pacific. Her prince would fly forth on the wings of an eagle and slay the dragons of the Orient who were threatening their kingdom. He would return, and they would build their palace. Helyanthe was divinely happy. Yes, fairy tales do come true! She got a local job, settled down in San Diego, and awaited his return.

It was Robert Burns who wrote:

> The best-laid schemes o' Mice an' Men,
>   Gang aft agley,
> An' lea'e us naught but grief an' pain,
>   For promis'd joy!

Six weeks later came a fateful telegram: "We regret to inform you that Lt. Robert Verner was lost in action while serving his country." Twice within the brief span of her young life, she had lost the one person on whose love she could depend.

Helen learned later that he was the pilot of a fighter plane. In a squadron battling Japanese bombers his was shot down. His comrades saw it strike the sea. Although some of the pilots so downed were rescued, he was not, and his body was never found.

She was again devastated, her dreams dashed. She was not superstitious, but it made her think that if you loved somebody, you would lose them. Love was dangerous. It hurt terribly. Dare she ever love again?

Helen rarely talked about Bob to me except to reiterate how much he was like Grossvater. One time, many years later, while digging through an old trunk she found his last letter. She cried on my shoulder as she read it to me. I cried with her.

Her dream of a castle on the mountain never came to pass. But on a Pacific hillside overlooking a beautiful island, there is a memorial park, called The Punch Bowl, where among the heroes of America there is carved in marble the name of Lt. Robert Verner.

Jack and Helen at a formal function, 1976.

HOPE AND DISILLUSIONMENT

Although she was grieving the loss of her two greatest loves, Helen knew she must get an advanced education and find her proper career. The family could now afford to send her to Penn State University, and a perusal of the catalogue reassured her it offered a strong pre-med curriculum. She would go there, register, and start training to become a medical doctor and help people.

However, she found there were many problems confronting a young war widow. It was the end of her first semester. She was wrestling with beginning anatomy when another pre-med student remarked, "Next year you get to do an autopsy."

"Autopsy? What's that?" she queried anxiously

"You know, you dissect cadavers—the bodies of dead people."

"You mean you cut into dead people's bodies?" she gasped in horror. She had never considered this possibility. She wanted to help people, not cut into their dead bodies. In her mind, doctors simply determined diagnoses, prescribed drugs, and made people well.

"Do I have to dissect cadavers to be a doctor?"

"Of course," replied the other with a frown. It sounded almost as if he thought she was stupid.

❦

The next day Hely entered the dean's office. "Sir, I want to change my major from pre-med. I don't want to be a doctor."

"What do you want to change it to?" inquired the sympathetic dean, scratching his graying hair.

"Well, I don't know. I just know I don't want to be a doctor."

The dean appraised her with a critical glance, peering over the top of his horn-rimmed bifocals. He already knew her excellent academic abilities. "You seem confused. Maybe you better go to the counseling center. They can help you decide." Helen retreated, wondering what she should become—not an opera diva, not a doctor, now what?

The next day she knocked on a somewhat forbidding door at the counseling center. The sign read: Jacob Wilberforce, Psychologist. A pasty-faced young man greeted her without enthusiasm. It had been a boring day trying to be cheerleader for five failing students.

Helen wondered how competent he was. He would determine her life career.

"I want to find out what major I should take," she volunteered. He moved to a large green file standing against the plain wood wall and extracted some folders from it.

"Take a desk in the next room—over there, and fill these out," he sighed while handing her a large envelope filled with papers.

She noted the heading on the first one: "Bernreuter Personality Inventory," the second, "Strong Interest Inventory," followed by a test of mental abilities. She recognized it. She had cracked ones like that many times, often breaking the ceiling. After filling them out rapidly, she handed them to him. He must be very important.

"I'll have these scored by tomorrow. Come back in the morning at ten," he said rather unenthusiastically while putting on his jacket and preparing to close up for the day.

The young man seemed rather surprised the next morning when she reported in and sat quietly, waiting her fate. These tests would tell her exactly what she was suited for. The young man, blinking through nearsighted glasses, studied the score sheets. He squirmed in his chair and seemed to be very confused. "Well, uh! You've got so many high scores in so many different fields you can do just about anything you want."

Helen thought, *You Dummkopf, I already know that.* Could he tell her which one would be the best? He had nothing much to say. The interview from then on rapidly descended to nowhere.

She rose, said politely, "Thank you," and left.

On the way back to the dorm she kept mulling the experience over in her mind. Then an exciting idea occurred to her: *I can give all those tests better than he can. He's supposed to be a psychologist. You just give the tests, find out all about people, then proceed to help them. That's what I'll be, a psychologist.*

She was so excited she raced up the stairs to her room on the dorm's second floor and called her family in Pittsburgh. "Mutter, I want to be a psychologist. I'm going to register tomorrow as a major in that field."

Anna was surprised. Psychologist? What was a psychologist? Oh yes, somebody who took care of insane people. What would this crazy little daughter of hers think of next: Actress, opera singer, doctor, and now psychologist? She would have to talk it over with Uncle George.

That evening her mother, Uncle George, and Aunt Mary discussed the matter. Anna was dubious, and Mary thought the idea was ridiculous. Guarding crazy people in asylums? What kind of a real job was that? George, however, who was more widely read in such matters, had a number of things to say.

"They do more than just take care of insane patients, Mary. They not only give psychological tests, but they work in general hospitals and mental health centers, and give counseling to ordinary people who have problems. I understand it's a coming field. If that's what she wants why not let her go for it?"

Mary grumped, "Might as well approve. She'll do it anyway."

The matter was settled. Anna called back and gave Helen the family blessing. She would be a psychologist.

Being a war widow was not easy for the young sophomore who was still mourning her personal losses, but she studied hard for the next three years. Almost all her grades were A's, and when she graduated she was awarded membership in Phi Beta Kappa, the honor society.

Helen sent her outstanding scholastic record together with rave recommendations from her enthusiastic professors to a number of schools having graduate programs in clinical psychology. She had acceptances from several but chose the University of Denver, which offered a full-ride scholarship. It would pay all her expenses through the doctorate. Besides, getting away to a new place in the West promised some change.

Then, within a year, another blow came without warning. Helen hadn't been told that her mother was suffering from ovarian cancer. Everybody had conspired to keep it from her, fearing that she would come rushing home and stop her graduate training. So it was another shock for which she was not prepared when she was informed of Mutter's death. One tragedy after another. Within a short period she had suffered the loss of the three most important people in her life: Grossvater, her husband Bob, and now her mother. How could she rise above this triple blow of fate? Could she ever dare to invest affection in another person?

Perhaps it was the depression, perhaps her need for somebody to whom she could talk, or perhaps just loneliness. But at the University of Denver she had met another graduate student, Richard Huth. He did not rouse in her the feelings she had experienced toward romantic Bob, or caring Grossvater, or the closeness she had with Mother. But he was somebody, and he was there. They were thrown together in many of the same classes. So they started keeping company. Richard (Dick) was developing a brief, rapid intelligence test, which could do a quick screening. She volunteered to help him with the research statistics and write some of the items. His thesis was accepted by the department, and he received a master's degree.

Helen undertook a more comprehensive research thesis involving the analysis of some one thousand interview protocols. As a result she, too, received a master's degree. They decided that practicing together in psychology might be a rewarding career for both of them—so they got married.

Helen became pregnant before she fully recognized that this man was not at all like Bob or Grossvater. With considerable dismay she realized she had made a mistake, but a baby was coming—and after that there was one more. German women, as well as men, do their duty. She must make the best of the situation and ensure that her children would have a father. Perhaps her lack of a father was part of her motivation.

It had been difficult through her childhood, when asked about her father, to always say, "He died." Other kids had dads, why didn't she? But Grosspapa almost made up for it. She knew she must stick it out until her children were grown and independent.

Dick was unreliable, given to beer drinking, and had difficulty holding a job. She found it necessary to supplement the family income with a part-time position as a physician's lab assistant. She was determined that her children would not want or be neglected.

Dick gave them little attention. It was her responsibility to be both mother and father to them. The marriage deteriorated into screaming matches. Dick never pursued a career in psychology but took a routine federal job. The future did not look promising.

He was transferred to Missoula, Montana, with a position in the Social Security Administration. Helen was fighting almost impossible odds to support her children and be a loving parent. The burden became overwhelming. She resigned from the clinical program at the university before completing her doctor's degree and moved to Missoula. She would reunite her family and try to rebuild a household. However, love had departed. Dick was more interested in drinking beer with his buddies.

She landed a job as a counselor in the University of Montana Counseling Center, a very rewarding position where she could use her natural talents and psychological training. After her son had joined the Air Force, and her daughter was in college, she and Dick were divorced. His only request for agreeing to the legal separation was that she bake a certain special German cake he liked once each year. She settled into life as a single mother raising two children.

Although there were men who sought her company, she kept them on the light side. Why risk being hurt again? She had been in love and lost. She had married twice and had lost. Now she would concentrate on being a good mother and developing her counseling skills. What more was there?

Helen on the day of her marriage to Jack, 1971.

The Crown Prince of Bavaria

It was only a hint, a very slight hint, and never until recently did I recognize it as fore-shadowing my future.

I and my family had just moved to Missoula, Montana. The school had hired me to organize and direct a doctoral training program in clinical psychology. What a challenge!

My wife didn't really want to leave Portland, where I was chief of the psychology service at the veterans hospital. And my children were not enthusiastic. Their schools and friends were back in Oregon where we had a nice home on Lake Oswego. But I had been offered a professorship at the University of Montana and a chance to develop a doctoral program in clinical psychology. Reluctantly my wife agreed to move.

The dean of letters and science at the university scheduled a meeting of all those concerned with mental health training. Plans would be discussed. Their new clinical director would be introduced.

At the long table sat a dozen persons. After I was properly presented, each individual, starting on my left, introduced him/herself. The last was a lady on my right. She said simply, "Helen Huth, counseling center." I nodded. She smiled.

When the meeting finished we were the last two to leave. I walked across the campus with her and chatted—some mundane things about Missoula weather. Then we went our separate ways, since the psychology department and the counseling center were quite distant from each other. Being engrossed with planning my new office, I forgot all about her.

That was it. No planting of a romantic urge; no sudden love story surge of passion, not even a flicker of further interest. If I had been told, "This is your future wife—with whom you will have a thirty-year honeymoon," I would have dismissed the idea as ridiculous. Not that she was unattractive. I just hadn't taken a second look. I was married, and I had a doctoral program to build.

During the next six years the psychology department and the counseling center were on parallel courses but with little interaction. Once in a while a psychology student was assigned to practicum at the center and came under Helen's supervision.

March 15. Wow, a card! "The Counseling Center invites you to a St. Patrick's Day coffee and refreshment. We understand it's your birthday." It was signed, "Helen Huth." How the devil did the center know my birthday? I went to the refreshment meeting—and took that second look.

By that time my marriage was on the rocks. My wife and I were steadily growing apart. What I saw at the counseling center that day was an attractive, smiling lady who seemed to listen to me when I talked. Interest planted. Nothing more.

During the following year, Helen and an associate of hers took my course in hypnotherapy. She was impressed and immediately incorporated this modality into her practice at the center.

By the next March my personal situation was changed. After fruitless attempts at reconciliation, I (with the concurrence of my wife) had initiated divorce proceedings. I moved out of our house, and was living in a rented basement room.

Helen and I got closer together, and by July I asked her to marry me. She seemed very warm but was noncommittal. She wanted assurance on two points:
1. Was there still a lingering attachment to my wife (perhaps I would return to her)?
2. Was she, Helen, really an American now—or was she still at heart a Bavarian?

On the first point she treated me as if I were a client in marital therapy, exploring and urging me to make every attempt at reconciliation—attempts that were rebuffed by my wife, who found too many things wrong with me, and I didn't know how to change them.

We had married in wartime on the rebound from previous unhappy relationships. But we had reared four children of whom we were proud, and my wife was a good mother to them. However, our personal relationship had declined over the years. She involved herself intensely in home and children, while I pursued an ambitious professional career. Now, neither of us met the needs of the other.

In August, Helen planned a trip to Bavaria to explore her Germanic roots. She might not return.

Perhaps when you are about to lose something, it becomes even more attractive. I had to make her want to come back. Neither just a basket of roses, nor an "I love you" letter, would do. However, she had evinced interest in my writings, including my poetry—and we were both romanticists. I would write a book of poems for her.

Purchasing a blank book, I set to a month before she was scheduled to leave and, almost filling it, presented it to her on our way to the airport. She promised to read it on the plane. (Later she told me it was a dirty trick.) She didn't even get a chance to see Bavaria again before she had decided to return. Helen was so modern in some ways, and so Victorian in others. If I wanted to move out of my basement room, it would be convenient for her if I lived in her house and took care of it while she was gone. However, she made it quite clear that when and if she returned I was to move out.

For over a month I sat in it alone, miserably confused, hoping, and playing over and over a Ray Conniff record, "Days of Wine and Roses." It became my symbol for loneliness. Little did I know I would be playing it again—thirty years later.

Bavaria: She visited her brother (Siegfried) and other relatives. She also wrote me friendly/affectionate letters with no commitment. As a successful physician Siegfried was in the best social circles and took her to a whirlwind of events, including the meeting of a culture society devoted to the preservation of Bavarian literature. Many prominent local story writers and poets were there presenting readings from their books.

Suddenly, the um-pah band struck up a strident march. Everyone immediately rose and stood at attention. Helen, looking around, wondered what was going on. She was told it was the Bavarian national anthem.

In strode a tall, handsome fellow in *lederhosen**—probably in his forties. Had I been there I would have been sure that all was lost. He was the crown prince of Bavaria. How could I compete with that? Helen was told that he was an attorney—apparently a good stepping-stone to political power in Germany, as in the United States.

Bavaria had been defeated by Prussia in 1970 and integrated into the German empire. However, it continued to maintain its nobility until Germany's defeat in 1918. Then, like the German Kaiser, the Bavarian king, Ludwig III, was forced to abdicate.

Bavaria, however, still had a royal family, and succession was determined by birth—as before. Some hoped that perhaps (maybe, you never know) the crown prince would be called again to resume the throne of his ancestors. Many of those hopeful Bavarians were present—in fact, everyone

---

*Leather pants

there stood at attention when the band played the national anthem. Where other than at a meeting devoted to Bavarian *Kultur* would this tradition have been continued?

The situation was: Helyanthe returns to Bavaria, visits the home of her childhood, is welcomed by friends and relatives, meets her handsome prince (the knight on the white horse), falls in love, and marries him. I would be alone.

But no! Fate had other plans. Helen was delighted to meet the prince, was entranced, had him autograph a Bavarian book she had bought, and planed her return to America—where she now knew she belonged.

Ever after, we would tell the story with much laughter. I would claim bragging rights as having outjousted the crown prince of Bavaria—and won the fair hand of Helen. Fairy tales do come true.

When Helen returned she brought back a little book, which she presented to me. It was entitled *Springs of Persian Wisdom*. She had bought it in a monastery near the Vienna Woods. On each right-hand page was a motive symbol in color and words of wisdom from Omar Khayyam or other ancient poets.

On the left page of each she had inscribed a reaction, reply, or comment. I read it through several times and was fascinated, not fully realizing then what a treasure trove it contained about the personhood of my sweetheart, and what she was telling me therein about herself.

I was overcome with joy when on the last page I read what she had written:

> And now for a final reaction—not to a printed verse, but to a letter you wrote me last July for my birthday—a very important letter proposing marriage.
>
> My reaction to that great and beautiful letter is a very simple and very humble, Yes! I love you, and I want no other man is this

world for a husband but you. If the offer still
stands I shall try to be to you whatever it is
I am capable of being.

Hely

After our marriage the little book was buried in a drawer and forgotten. I rediscovered it thirty years later, after I
had lost her.

Helen's untraditional and unique differences showed
from the very beginning of our relationship. After her
acceptance of my proposal it was agreed that we were
engaged. Not trusting my own judgment, I suggested we go
together to the jewelers where I would buy her the exact ring
she wanted. When we arrived at the store I asked, "What do
you have in engagement rings?"

The merchant smiled and reached into the showcase.
Helen suddenly announced, "I don't want a diamond; I want
a pearl." He and I were both surprised.

"Well, uh, I don't have any engagement rings with pearls
in them, but I can make one special for you."

What Hely wants, Hely gets. She wore the engagement
ring the rest of her life—except when the pearl twice needed replacing.

At the wedding she pulled another surprise. We had
agreed to write the ceremony together. It would be partly in
English and partly in German. The Lutheran minister could
speak German, and we wrote the exact wording. The music
was the wedding march from *Lohengrin*. I would give my say-
ings in English, and she would speak hers in German. Her
son, Marvin, would give her away.

> After we had pledged our troth to each
> other, Helen, in her Bavarian accent had
> said:
> Ich, Helen, geboren Helyanthe, nahme
> Dich, Johann, als meinen Ehegatten, von
> dieser Stunde an: fur was auch immer das

Schicksal bringen mag, ob sonnige oder
trube Zeiten, ob kranke oder gesunde Tage,
und nur Dich allein, in Liege und Vertrauen,
bis zum letzten Tage unseres Lebens
zusamen.*

We had decided against a double-ring ceremony, so after
I placed the ring on her finger, there was an unplanned space
for a comment by her. The program on which we had agreed
merely labeled it, "Remarks by Helen." I had not asked her
just what she intended to say. She then spoke as follows:

I have no ring to give to you and pledge of
my abiding love. Instead, I give you my hand
to symbolize my commitment to you. But I
make this commitment to you only for
today, because tomorrow is not within my
power to give.

A gasp swept over the gathering. Several shocked people
whispered to each other, "She's only pledging to be true to
him for one day—today!" Even I was surprised.

After only a slight hesitation, but in a firm voice, Helen
proceeded with her unrevealed script.

"Since tomorrow is never here, I can only pledge myself
to you today. But, you see, as I renew my pledge to you each
day, then every day will become a new wedding day."

She was right. Every day from then on for the next thirty years was for us a new wedding day.

---

*I Helen, born Helyanthe, take thee, John, as my lawful husband, from
this hour forward: for whatever fate may bring, in sunny or troubled times,
in sickness or health, and with you alone in closeness and trust, until the
last days of our life together.

Jack and Helen at her daughter's wedding, 1982.

WISDOM OF THE ANCIENT PERSIANS

The little book that Helen brought back from her trip to Bavaria, and which she gave to me, was only three inches by five inches in size. It had a gorgeous cover in gold and red, which could have been the pattern of a fine Persian rug. I was so eager to read it that at the time I did not realize the air of antiquity and profound wisdom that its jacket conveyed. On the first page she had written:

> Lieber Hans:
>
> In a monastery book store by the Vienna Woods I picked up this English-written booklet of Persian wisdom. I bought it because I understandably liked it, and now I want to give it to you for a specific purpose. Read each printed verse first then my handwritten reactions. I want to share these reactions with you—all of them even unto the last page.
>
> Hely

I could not conceive then of the profound messages it would convey, nor of its deep meanings in her own heart. Even the place where she acquired it, a Viennese monastery, bespoke a higher, religious aspect. But it was only now, thirty years later, after I had lost her, that I have studied the poems and the responses she had inscribed.

That little book of poems and her inscriptions obviously would let me know whether she would marry me. So I read it, just as she requested. I did not, like an eager child, turn immediately to the last page to see how the story would all come out. (It was difficult to overcome my impatience, though.)

Helen, with her sensitive understanding, had already decided that I was the one for her. But before making commitments she wanted to let me know more about herself, her own personhood, just what I would be getting. Accordingly, she even wrote on the last page of the little book, "If the offer still stands [as if she didn't know], then I accept."

I read through every page carefully before the last. But there are times when we have eyes but do not see, or ears but do not hear. I did not then apprehend her truly deep and sensitive messages—and the book was buried in a drawer for the following thirty years.

Now, reading it almost as if for the first time, I realize how much it revealed of her philosophy of life, religion, love, sex, human understanding, her very essence, her selfhood. It was as if she had absorbed the wisdom of the ancients and then added her own. Much of that wisdom is exemplified in the stories of her life described in these chapters. But I will reveal a few of the jewels from the little book to illustrate her thinking just before she married me. The following are excerpts from the Persian poems (left) followed by her reactions (right).

PERSIAN POEM	HELEN'S REACTION
Do not seek, and do not expect these three things for you will seek them in vain. A man of knowledge whose deeds correspond with his knowledge, a man of action whose heart accords with his deeds, and a fellow human being with no failings.	And do not expect perfection from me, for then you will be disappointed.
Through love all things become lighter which understanding thought too heavy.	Through your love the impossible becomes possible, and the burdens of life become lighter.
I have firmly resolved never to drink wine again! And if thirst plays me no tricks, I shall hold to it.	It is hard to resist my vices, but with your help I might try, providing the torte is not too tempting.
Do not condemn you neighbor out of hand. Be generous, forgive, pardon. If each knew everything about the other, he would forgive gladly and easily. There would be no more pride, no more arrogance.	It is hard if not impossible to hate someone that you really get to know and understand. That is why I stay away from people I want to dislike.

PERSIAN POEM	HELEN'S REACTION
If a word burns on your tongue, so let it burn.	Yes, so you are reminded of your own humanity with all of its inevitable foibles. To believe that one can rise above one's own humanity is to play at being God. Such play is dangerous.
Everything that happens and everything that befalls us has meaning, but it is often difficult to recognize it. Also in the book of life every page has two sides: We human beings fill the upper side with our plans, hopes and wishes, but Providence writes on the other side. And what it ordains is seldom our goal.	I see our meeting in this world as an act of Providence, Kismet, a happening, the meaning of which we did not recognize two years ago. Hopefully our plans and those of Providence coincide.
Kindness can charm a snake from its hole.	To be kind is to care, and only through caring can one reach another soul.

PERSIAN POEMS	HELEN'S REACTION
But while the Eternal One created me, He word by word, spelt out my lesson, love, and seized my heart and from a fragment cut keys to the storehouse of reality.	Ah yes, yes! Love is real. It is the only reality that has real meaning. It opens the door of life. It cures, it heals, it is the antithesis of death.
A gourd of red wine, and a sheaf of poems—a bare subsistence, half a loaf, not more—supplied us two alone in the free desert. What sultan could we envy on his throne?	Hmm! How beautiful our picnics along Rock Creek with bread and wine and us.
Do you know what can never be satisfied? The eye of greed. All the world's goods cannot fill the abyss of its desire.	And I have felt greed in operation here in Europe, and it makes me weep. It makes me weep in America too; but somehow the pain is closer here because Europe represents my childhood to me, and childhood should be innocent.

Helen had returned to Bavaria for the first time since she had left it as a child before World War II, before Hitler. She had high hopes, but its industrialization, the dependence on foreign labor, and the striving for money had changed this fairy tale country. Perhaps this had some bearing on her conclusion that she was now truly an American and belonged here in Montana—with me.

PERSIAN POEMS	HELEN'S REACTION
If an angel sits down with the devil, he learns cunning deceit and evil. Those who associate with evil learn no good—one does not learn to sew pelts from the wolf.	But if the devil sits down with an angel can there be no positive influence? Seems sad that we human beings consider the bad to be a temptation and therefore something desirable, and the good not a temptation (and therefore not desirable). By this logic we should teach children to be bad so that the good is tempting. We humans are a strange lot.

Helen didn't believe in good and evil. She believed in good, and dismissed evil, probably because she had never experienced it in her life. Her existence was largely spent in dispensing affection and understanding to others, even as she was the recipient of much love from those who had been her clients.

In her early years as a counselor, it was the college students whom she rescued. Later, as she became a psychotherapist, her practice consisted largely of mental health practitioners (psychiatrists, psychologists, counselors) who came to her for personal problems and to improve their own therapeutic skills.

She would mobilize her therapeutic self and transmit its attitudes to these professional clients. They usually left the intensive weekend consultations with her feeling better about themselves and their abilities as therapists in treating others.

Helen thought of evil as destructive behavior, destructive of both the perpetrator and his victims. The evil one could be rehabilitated, and it was her goal to find the good within and bring it out, and help the individual mobilize this inner strength to become a guiding factor in his life.

In thinking of cases, she would constantly ask herself, *What are his/her inner strengths? How can they be mobilized?* And that is how she would conceptualize her patients. She would seek such resources in her professional clients and teach them how to find them in their patients. She knew there was always a therapeutic ego state in these clients or they would not be in business as mental health professionals. This belief sometimes led to creative and amusing conceptions.

One can almost visualize her innovative mind clicking as follows: *It is the job of the angel to discover the latent good in the devil, rehabilitate him and release it. Then he will leave their session changed—going forth in the world to do good for people.* And you know just whom she had in mind as the angel to do that job.

She then, almost facetiously, suggested that by reversing the connections of temptation to the bad we can use it to turn normal human motivations in the direction of the good.

PERSIAN POEMS

Water does not stay in a sieve, nor gold in a generous pocket. Nor patience in love. Let him be patient who can! Be content with three glasses of pure wine. And if three are not granted you, then drink one gladly. Learn from the juice of the grape which fills the three glasses that life is a trinity of heart, soul and mind.

HELEN'S REACTION

While here in Europe these six weeks I learned to appreciate more of what I have in my work, my home, my family, friends, and particularly in you.

PERSIAN POEMS	HELEN'S REACTION
He is nearest to self-knowledge and self-realization who accepts his lot contentedly, for contentment is man's happiness, even in the bitterness of daily life.	I am content, but then I have good reason to be. I have you.

This is her last message before inscribing her beautiful acceptance of my marriage proposal. It changed my life forever.

And now I must learn to be content even with the bitterness of daily life brought on by her loss. I must learn from her.

*Helen in one of her wigs,
dressed up for an evening out with Jack.*

CRAZY-MAKING AND
OTHER LUNACIES

Helen enjoyed competitive games, and she was very good at them, often winning. But she would never hurt or humiliate her opponent. It was more like playing, winning, laughing, and then hugging each other.

In high school I had belonged to a checkers and chess club, had been number one in checkers, and near the top in chess. I did not realize that Helen also played chess, but early in our marriage the matter of playing the game for recreation arose.

I soon found that Helen was good—very, very good. She beat me five games in a row. She used logical German tactics and took one piece of mine after another. It was like General von Ludendorff's strategy in 1918 when he bulldozed his great offensive toward Paris. How could I counter such Teutonic thoroughness? I decided on an extreme method: crazy-making.

Crazy-making is a neurotic technique that couples often play against each other. From clients in her counseling practice, Helen had shown me that it occurred where winning was more important than the feelings of the other. It is recipe for a failing marriage and typically goes like this:

Husband is disturbed because wife is spending too much money. He chides her and explains logically just why she should economize. He is right. Husband wins? No!

Wife makes crazy. She cries, accuses him of not loving her, of being stingy, not like he was when he was courting her. Sometimes she throws in a below-the-belt clincher by comparing his income-making ability unfavorably to that of her brother. He sullenly retreats. Wife wins? Yes-No! Both lose. The marriage is headed toward disaster.

But since I couldn't beat Helen in a fair chess game, I decided to try some crazy-making. After she had brilliantly established a position designed to trap me into a checkmate, I would start trading like mad, first our queens, then our rooks, then every other piece. Was the tactic successful? Completely. Wow! She would get mad at me, lose the game, and demand that I play chess like civilized people—according to the rules. So, had I won the game? Yes-No!

It was not good for one of us to win all the time, but it was destructive of love to crazy-make. Without discussing the matter, we apparently decided mutually this situation did not promote happiness in our marriage. After that we never played chess anymore; we would compete in other ways. In card games, like hearts or pinochle, she often won, but not always. But for both of us the competition was then fun.

※

In the university counseling center Helen's two closest friends were Jim and Fred. Fred was the center's director. He had originally come as a graduate student and was supervised by Helen. After finishing his doctorate, he stayed on as staff and ultimately became its director (her boss).

I first met Fred when he was a graduate assistant to Helen, and I was courting her. I was a consultant with the Montana State Prison, and he was doing a practicum there. He was also completing his doctoral dissertation and was having trouble with it. He asked Helen for suggestions, and she advised him as follows, "Why don't you ask Dr. Watkins for some help with the problem? He works a lot with student dissertations."

Fred replied, "I did, but I couldn't get any help from him."

Helen seemed puzzled. "How come? I've never known him to refuse helping a student before."

It was Fred's turn to look confused. "He and I go to the prison on the same day, and we often share a ride together. So I decided to bring up the problem one evening when we were returning from Deer Lodge."

"Yes! And what did he do?"

"He didn't do anything. All he did was talk about you. Every time I asked a question about my dissertation he would change the subject and start talking again about Helen."

During the following years Fred, having completed his doctorate, was hired by the counseling center as a staff member. He demonstrated administrative skills, and when Helen, who simply wanted to do therapy, refused an offer to become the center's director, Fred was given the job.

With Jim, Helen had an affectionate love-hate battle going. The game was to see who could insult the other most. It was continued over the years to the accompaniment of much laughing.

One time the telephone sounded in Helen's office. "Helen, this is Jim. Could you return that special report which required our opinions?"

Helen slyly replied, "I put it in the left-hand top drawer of your desk, Jim." There were a few moments of silence. Then a loud yell reverberated throughout the center. Helen doubled up with peals of laughter.

Moments later, Jim burst out of his office holding up a finger, a very red finger. She had set a mousetrap in his desk drawer. After a period of curses and invective, Jim quieted down. No great harm had been done. Over the years they both told of the incident and laughed.

Several years later, Helen and I were presenting a workshop in Mexico City when she suddenly announced, "I need to go shopping. Jim's birthday is coming up, and I promised to send him something from Mexico."

We threaded through the crowded streets past a number of stalls selling colorful blankets until we reached the city's fish market. Many varieties of fresh seafood were openly displayed. Helen walked slowly through these stalls, inspecting each carefully. Finally she came to a stall featuring very ugly and grotesque devilfish. Helen selected a particularly large and smelly one, saying, "I'll take this one. Wrap it up!" The gray-haired woman, wearing a bright colored shawl, promptly obeyed.

Then Helen asked in bad Spanish, "Is there anyplace around here where I can get fancy, colorful gift wrap?" The woman looked as if she couldn't believe what this crazy Gringo lady was doing with fancy gift wrap. She pointed down the street.

A few blocks further on we found a gift shop. While giggling, Helen picked out a very expensive, gaily colored sheet that featured the expression, "Felix Annivariso." Chuckling all the time, she inscribed a note that read, "Thinking of you. Love, Helen." Little Hely was having a field day.

A clerk at a nearby post office duly affixed air mail stamps, and the package was sent off addressed to Dr. James Wemple, University of Montana Counseling Center, Missoula, Montana. I never heard just what happened when the package arrived and was opened, probably at a staff meeting—but I could guess.

Although Helen liked to win, to tease and surprise her friends, she also had quite a sense of fair play—even when it was not to her advantage.

One day, a local Dixieland band, The Town-Gown Music Appreciation Society, in which I, an amateur clarinetist, played, had the opportunity to recruit an excellent, experienced clarinet man.

Realizing that now I was not needed, I wondered what new instrument I might take up that would contribute to the combo. That night I dreamed of making a vibraphone out of sticks. One of my jazz heroes, Lionel Hampton, played the vibraphone. *Ah-hah!* I thought. *That's what I'll learn to play.*

Of course to start, I would get a small one with a limited range, but one that would be adequate to determine whether I was suited to that instrument. I discovered that a vibraphone was not to be found in Missoula. Hearing that a woman, a concert artist in Spokane, had one for sale, I visited her. Perhaps hers would be small, and I could buy it inexpensively. For support, I appreciated Helen's accompanying me.

We were met at the door by a pleasant-looking lady with slightly graying hair. "Yes, I have both a vibraphone and a marimba. I want to sell one of them."

We were invited in. There in the middle of the living room sat a large, concertmaster, gold-plated, Musser vibraphone. I gasped! It looked wonderful, but could I afford it? I sounded the lady out and got an idea of the approximate amount she wanted—several thousand dollars—so I told her I'd think about it, and we left.

I thought about it and thought about it. The more I thought, the more I wanted it. Finally, at Helen's urging I went back to Spokane, again taking her with me—since women are better at bargaining than men. And just to make sure, I took in cash the amount I knew the lady wanted— minus $500. The bargaining went as follows:

"I can afford —— amount, and I have it here in cash to pay you now."

She smiled and replied, "That's not enough for such a fine instrument in perfect condition. I want —— for it."

I don't give up easily. "Well! This is what I can pay you right now, today."

She smiled again and said, "You heard my price." (Did I detect a slight weakening in her resolve? Should I continue pressing her?) I didn't get to test this theory.

At that point Helen stepped in to help me out. "Jack! Don't be such a cheapskate. You want it, and you know it's worth that. Pay the lady what she asks!"

The bargaining ceased, and we went home with the elegant, gold-plated, concert-model Musser vibraphone securely lashed in our truck. Need it be said that I never again took Hely to help me bargain.

❧

Helen also delighted in springing surprises, especially on those she loved. They were unexpected, sometimes amazing, and she would spare no trouble or expense in arranging them.

One day, while we were strolling along a busy street in Chicago, I noticed a large bookstore. A bookstore is for me like cheese is for a rat. Whenever I went to a bookstore Helen would say with a disapproving look, "Now don't buy more books. You've got several unread ones sitting on the table already."

In the store's large display window there were several very interesting and enticing offerings. Helen patiently waited for me to finish licking my chops, but I didn't go in. As we walked on toward our convention hotel I casually mentioned, "I see that Britannica has just put out a new edition." I already had an older set, left to me by my father when he died. It was out of date but still usable. Helen said no word, and the moment faded from my attention as we walked briskly toward our hotel.

Two weeks later American Express delivered a large, heavy box to our porch. *What could that possibly be?* I wondered. I should have guessed.

Helen was snickering while I opened the box. It was a set of the new encyclopedia. I was floored, and Helen convulsed in laughter, then eagerly puckered up her lips to get my kisses and thank-yous.

Not all her gifts were equally welcome. Helen's daughter, Karen, was also a clinical psychologist. Once, when she and her husband had been offered positions at a clinic in Alaska, they were preparing to drive three thousand miles up the long Canadian highway to Soldotna. Their station wagon was bulging with bags, clothing, and other goods they would need to furnish the house they intended to acquire there.

Karen's son Sascha was already in the backseat, and Gene, her husband, was starting the car when Helen drove up to say "Good-bye." She had brought a going-away present. It was an owl totem pole, carved by a local artist from a five-foot pine log, one foot in diameter, and so heavy I could barely lift it. The rest of us were shocked. I wondered what Karen and Gene would do with it.

The matter was settled. The gift was lifted on top of the station wagon and secured with ropes, and the little family drove off heading for the first stop in Alberta on the way to Alaska. Helen was very pleased with herself.

But the most astounding surprise occurred during the annual convention of a scientific society to which Helen and I had long been contributing members. The meeting was in Asheville, North Carolina. We had prepared a joint paper to present, but just before we left Missoula, Helen received a call from a patient who was in a crisis situation, and who requested immediate therapy sessions. To Helen, a distress signal from one of her patients had the highest priority; she canceled her plan to accompany me to the convention, and I was left to travel there alone.

The meeting was rather dull. Our paper was greeted with polite applause. The last session of the three-day conference arrived. At the morning break I returned to my hotel room and called Helen. It would be eight o'clock in Missoula. "Hi, Liebchen, are you up, or did I wake you?"

"Of course not, Dummkopf. I'm always up before you. Did you present our paper?"

"Yeah! But they announced that the presentation was by Helen and Jack Watkins. I had to explain to them why you weren't here. Did you really have to see that patient? Couldn't she wait until next week? You belonged here with me!"

"Well, Darling, I know you were your usual brilliant self, and the paper was enthusiastically received. I spent all yesterday with the patient. She'll be OK."

I grumbled to myself, "Of course, she would be OK. They always are—once they've seen Helen."

"Just wanted to know everything was going well with you. Love you, Dear! I'm looking forward to being together again."

"I am, too," she remarked while hanging up the phone. How like her. She would greet me with open arms at the airport.

It was the last day of the convention. Without her beside me the papers seemed especially boring. So I took a guided tour of the Biltmore, that magnificent palace erected by the famous Vanderbilt family. The paintings adorning the marble halls were magnificent, but I was still bored.

At scientific conventions it is customary that on the last night a formal dinner is held. The presenters and attendees congregate in a large banquet hall, the gentlemen in dark suits, the ladies in formal gowns. Over glasses of wine and cocktails they exchange good-natured conversation for an hour. Then at eight o'clock dinner is announced. The big adjoining doors to the hotel ballroom are opened, and the crowd files in to be seated at the linen-covered tables guarded by stiff waiters in white jackets.

During the cocktail hour I had hoped to find one of our mutual friends to sit with, one who might be an interesting dinner companion, but found no one. So, near the back of the line, I resigned myself to finding some vacant seat, probably between two dull associates. In relative silence I would consume the ten-dollar chicken dinner for which the hotel had charged the convention price of fifty dollars.

Suddenly two of our close friends approached. "Jack, we've been looking for you. Would you join us and the Newtons (also close friends)? We've reserved a table."

How delightful, I thought. *I'm rescued.*

As we approached the designated table, there was one vacant chair, obviously reserved for me. I noticed from a distance that next to that seat was a beautiful blonde woman. I had a strange feeling of déjà vu.

As I approached my seat, the lady, elegantly attired in a gorgeous blue party dress, turned and looked at me. And with that sly, pixie-like, little-girl smile, which had always been able to melt me, my wife exclaimed, "Good evening, Sweetheart," pursing her lips for a kiss.

A roar of laughter broke over our dinner companions, which rapidly spread to nearby tables of friends and colleagues, as they were apprised of the situation.

Helen explained: "After your call this morning my patient canceled our session for today. Said she didn't need it. I thought, 'Wouldn't it be fun to surprise Jack?'"

She had then gotten a plane ticket at the last moment, arrived an hour before the banquet and, borrowing a room from a mutual friend, had prettied herself. Avoiding me while sneaking through the cocktail party, she had been seated at the table by our friends, who chuckled while they cooperated in the conspiracy.

We ate dinner together, jitterbugged and waltzed to the big sound band, then the next morning returned to Missoula. That was an evening I'd never forget. But then, that was my Hely.

❧

Sometimes Helen's surprises would go amiss. When her teenage daughter, Karen, returned from a vacation trip to

France, Helen put on a fiery red wig and excessive makeup, wore a tight-fitting short dress and boots, and looked just like a prostitute. Chuckling to herself, Helen waited in the baggage area near where Karen would retrieve her suitcases. The debarking travelers filed down the stairs. Karen approached, picked up her bag, took one look at her mother, and then said simply, "Hi, Mom," as she passed on.

Hely often dressed herself unusually, acted differently, and sometimes wore wigs—as she said, to keep me interested. I kept interested.

On the other hand she didn't want me to be unpredictable. She wanted me to be stable, a Rock of Gibraltar, always there when she needed me—like Grossvater.

Life with Hely was often bewildering—but it was never dull.

Dancing in Brazil.

STORM THE PALACE

At the university, Helen was recognized as the mother hen of the counseling center. The counselors, graduate students, and clerical staff at the center were a close-knit family, affectionate toward one another. Helen often helped the center's personnel with personal problems, love affairs, or other difficulties.

In every university there is a hierarchy of prestige, known affectionately as the pecking order. Departments that bring the most power, grant money, or public recognition, such as law, business, or the hard-core sciences, carry the most clout in administrative support. The counseling center was not one of these.

The center had been moved several times, from one temporary building or inconspicuous wing of a more permanent building after another—just any space not desired by higher-up entities. Finally, however, it had acquired its own bailiwick, an old white frame building on the edge of the campus that, many decades earlier, had been a private residence. Altered into little counseling cubicles, there were several real offices, and Helen, being the most senior staff counselor, occupied one of her own. There she had quietly hidden from administrative notice, rescuing distressed students.

This year as usual, the legislature, being more interested in cutting taxes, had not appropriated sufficient funds to run the university. It had also, as usual, told the university administration to make do by eliminating unessential programs. And the administration, as usual, was scurrying around looking for unessential programs."

A new vice president was recruited from a more prestigious school. He was reported to be an expert in fiscal efficiency, and would find the unessential programs.

It was the day after the beginning of Christmas break. Most of the students, happy to leave quarterly exams behind, had piled into cars and the few available planes. They had gone home to receive their justly deserved rewards from family and Santa Claus.

Unexpectedly, a memorandum was suddenly delivered by the new vice president to Fred, the center's director: "The Counseling Center is abolished, and all its staff members are hereby discharged, effective immediately. The psychiatrist in the Student Health Center has agreed to handle any student with *mental* problems."

The memorandum, probably at the suggestion of the new vice president, was timed to emerge when few students would be left on campus. They would return in January, be presented with the fait accompli and, after some grumbling, would no doubt accept it—or so the new vice president thought.

In the counseling center consternation reigned. Secretaries were crying. Graduate students in the midst of their practicums were devastated, and staff members started looking for jobs at other institutions. All were in a state of catastrophic emotions—all except Helen. She didn't seem unusually disturbed.

Helen was a lady of peace, whose business was providing help and understanding to students. She and the other counselors dealt daily with their little tragedies. Now the center was faced with its own survival.

She was very protective of "her" children. Anyone who attacked them immediately mobilized her defenses. Her biggest "child" of all, the counseling center, was now threatened with extinction.

Bismarck is quoted as saying, "We Germans fear God and nothing else on earth." He may have been talking about Helen. She was even prepared to rehabilitate Satan, and she had stood up to God's personal representative, the nun who had been her teacher. Besides, God was simply a big, benevolent father in the sky—like Grossvater. Therefore, why should she fear a mere university president?

A theory advanced by Carl Jung, the noted psychoanalyst, states that each of us have within our self a "contrasexed soul." He called the one in women animus, the one in men, anima. These were unconscious aspects of us that represented underlying strengths, and would determine (among other matters) how well one related to the opposite sex.

While there is no empirical evidence for their existence (and I am skeptical), I did have an interesting experience in personal psychoanalysis. During the early stages of my analysis with the good Dr. Weiss (who was trained by Freud), I would dream of a little crippled girl. At various times during the treatment she would appear older and healthier. And when I finished, after hundreds of hours on the couch, she was revealed in a final dream as a healthy, robust young woman. This presumably was my anima.

Likewise, Helen once described to me a dream image, which could have been her animus. It was a big, strong Hun, with horns on his helmet, carrying a huge shield and a broadsword.

Helen swung into action. She talked to a number of key students, explaining the memorandum and the consequences to them. They talked to other students, and they, to still others. A few idealistic orators in the dorms and fraternities organized groups and made impassioned pleas.

When the students returned in January the information spread through the campus like a Montana forest fire. "The counseling center, Helen, and the others are all being fired!" One must be careful in provoking a hornets' nest. A swarm of students demanded to see the president. His secretary was fending them off by the scores. Now, within the administrative offices of the CEO and his cabinet, consternation reigned. This riot must be stopped.

In any such organization, a system is usually in place to protect the chief, whether it be the president of a corporation, governor of a state, the president of the nation, a king, an emperor, or even a dictator. The chief must never be wrong or appear mistaken. Presidents don't change their minds. You can read every day in the political news from Washington, D.C. that policies are being reexamined. The final action (or compromise) is represented as a victory for the chief, who had previously planned it. Underlings are incompetent; they misinform the director, or misinterpret his policies. They can be fired. Did you ever hear of an executive simply admitting, "I goofed"?

A policy, already announced, needed reversing. Helen was invited to confer with the president.

Very relaxed, and the less anxious of the two, she came completely prepared. Politely she described in detail all the counseling services to individual students and groups, those who were rescued from academic failure, and those whose anxieties and psychosomatic disabilities impaired normal functioning.

She added pointedly that the center had averted several possible suicides. What would the president do if a student committed suicide, and the university were sued by parents for several million dollars—because it failed to provide protective counseling? What new enrollees would come to a university that was nationally reputed for not taking good, personal care of its students?

Helen also spent time describing the efficiency and excellent staff relations maintained by her colleague Fred.

The president thought. He thought very hard. More meetings of the administrative staff were held. Soon after that, a different (and more understanding) vice president approached Fred. "Can you put together a new proposal, embodying the most modern thinking about the organization of counseling services in universities?"

Fred and the vice president conferred at length. They came up with a new integrative concept, a center for student development. The formation of this new center was promptly announced by the administration with provisions as follows:

The staff of the counseling center would not be discharged, but would be augmented. The new center would be enlarged to include within its scope many additional programs for students, such as: admissions, career services, foreign students, handicapped students, black students, financial aid, academic advising, and veterans' affairs. Fred would be appointed director of this bigger operation and later designated director of student affairs, a position comparable to dean of students.

Everybody was pleased at this compromise. The riot subsided. The students returned to their studies. The president breathed easy—and resumed searching for unessential programs. The new vice president soon disappeared. The center's staff was delighted. Fred assumed increased responsibilities. Helen continued quietly treating students—and her Hun warrior animus returned to the dark forests of Bavaria.

Formal ball in Munich.

JACK AND HELEN

King Henry VIII had six wives. He wasn't pleased with some of them. So he divorced two and executed two. In Helen, I had at least six, but I was delighted with all of them. She said she wanted to give me a harem, keep me busy at home. She did.

I don't know whether that is a characteristic of German wives or simply Hely, since my experience with German wives ($N = 1$) does not permit me to generalize.

During the early years of our marriage she kept a cabinet full of wigs—all shapes and colors, and she delighted in surprises. The phone at my office in the psychology department would ring. "Jack, don't forget we're going to the Elks Club tonight. They're having a jazz band."

Of course. I knew they were having a jazz band, Glen Muller's Dixieland Combo (sometimes I jammed with them). They played all the old swing and jazz numbers Hely and I loved to dance to.

As a teenager I had matured late. The fifteen-year-old girls didn't want to date a cherub-faced thirteen-year-old with a high-pitched voice. So I had worked hard learning to dance well. That was my only ace. And Helen was a marvelous dancer.

But I never knew which wife would come from the bedroom when we were ready to leave. Sometimes she would close the door while deciding on the dress and hairdo. My pretty redhead of the day, who had been editing an article, could emerge as a blond bombshell for the evening.

⁂

Helen was always a lady. For every special date, she would go to the hairdresser, facial person, manicurist, or pedicurist—and I would tease her, "Well, is it your face, your hair, your fingernails, your toes—or your nose today?"

She would come back with, "You're such an Idaho hick, you wouldn't know good taste when you saw it."

And so it would go.

Whenever we went out, Helen insisted I wear a white shirt, jacket, and tie. Sometimes when we arrived at a gathering that turned out to be informal, the other men came in open shirts and blue jeans. I felt overdressed.

⁂

Helyanthe's childhood brimmed with castles and kings, knights and queens, and her fantasies were filled with opera melodies. If a familiar opera were playing whenever we were in New York or in Munich, we went.

In Salmon, Idaho, my father had sung the part of the captain in a local production of Gilbert and Sullivan's *H.M.S. Pinafore*, and I had played viola in high school and college orchestras, but grand opera was a new world to me.

When listening to an opera Helen would identify with the characters. This meant throwing herself into them as completely as she resonated with her patients. She knew most of the great operas well and could sing along with the major arias. She would often flood herself with tears and die with Carmen or Violetta, her favorites.

Every other year she attended courses in opera at the University of Innsbruck, Austria, where she met two teacher friends for the six-week summer sessions.

⁂

Once in Sydney, Australia, our tour group was late returning from a trip to Canberra. The bus driver had tried valiantly to get us to the opera—by cruising seventy miles an hour through the suburbs of Sydney. He didn't quite make it on time. The overture of Mozart's *The Magic Flute* had already started, and we were not admitted until after the first act. If Helen ever approached rage and violence it was at the Dummerlies among our tour companions who had been slow returning to the bus. You should hear German cussing.

As psychologists giving workshops, studying psychological theories, or treating patients, we may have been scientists, but in our personal life we were hopeless romantics, or maybe just starry-eyed adolescents—what you might call "corny."

Music was the food of our romance. We loved to dance together, especially to a big swing band. It took us back to our youthful days—World War II, before we had met each other. We could imagine we were together then.

I sometimes played the vibraphone that Helen had helped me buy—for $500 more than I wanted to pay. She liked its beautiful vibrato. In the evenings, while Helen was reading in bed, I would sometimes practice with recordings of Benny Goodman or Pete Fountain. When I was tired and prepared to quit, she might call from the bedroom, "Don't stop. I like it."

Then I would play a few more pieces, always finishing with one of our romantic numbers. We had two special ones: "I Left My Heart in San Francisco," as we had honeymooned in that beautiful city, and that oldie, "Love's Old Sweet Song." Playing one of those was the signal for intimate togetherness before we went to sleep. She knew that signal and eagerly awaited it.

Spring was coming early one particular Friday in mid-March. The lilacs on the big bush just outside the kitchen window were beginning to bloom. I was partly retired, but Helen was still working full-time at the counseling center.

On Fridays we often went out for breakfast, but for some reason, Helen said, "No. I'm fixing breakfast today." She cooked waffles, my favorite. This time they didn't stick in the waffle iron and break into pieces—as they usually did.

Helen seemed exceptionally loving today, kissing me on the back of the neck, or patting me every time she passed behind my chair. "Your dark blue suit is at the cleaners. Get it!"

"Sure—this afternoon."

Looking at me a little strangely, and in that occasional don't-you-forget voice (which brooked no argument), she snapped, "Be sure you do it!"

It was about three o'clock. I was completely involved in writing the first draft of a book chapter, when Helen opened the door to my study. "You better get that suit now. The cleaners will be closed soon."

I was in the middle of a hot inspiration and didn't want to break off. "The publisher wants this manuscript right away. Why don't I get the suit tomorrow?"

"No!" she said firmly. "Go get it now."

Grumbling, and wondering why all the rush, I asked, "Are we going someplace tonight?"

"I forgot to tell you. I've agreed for us to attend a dinner and dance tonight at the Red Lion." The Red Lion then was the biggest and fanciest hotel in town.

"What for?" I queried.

"It's a big charity."

"A charity for what?"

"Well, it's a . . ." She paused a moment. "I can't remember at the moment. Anyway, it's a big occasion, and I thought we ought to go."

I puzzled a moment then dropped the matter.

Helen's charities were quite a deal. I knew she had many, but it was not until after her death that I realized how many. There were: Crippled Children in Rwanda, Rescue the Palm Trees in the Holy Land, the Fund for Defending Free Speech, a high school girl in Sri Lanka, etc., etc.

We had two bank accounts: Hers and Ours. I deposited my university check in Ours. She deposited her state check and her private-practice money in Hers. By agreement, she was "Secretary of the Exchequer" and paid the bills, including our donations. The house bills came out of Ours. I never knew how she spent Hers.

Somewhat begrudgingly, I broke off my typing and retrieved the dark blue suit.

It was almost eight o'clock, and I, always time-oriented, was getting impatient. She seemed to be dragging her feet, with that interminable fixing her face, picking up books in the living room, and other unnecessary tasks. "Hurry up. We'll be late," I urged.

"Oh! It won't hurt if we're a bit late," she replied.

We drove to the hotel. All the parking places in the front lot were taken. Cruising around, we finally found a vacant one and then entered the building through a side door—then down a long corridor. Why is Helen walking so slow? I thought.

We arrived at the ballroom door. There was a bustle of activity going on inside. Several hundred people were sitting at tables. We entered.

Immediately, everyone stood up, looked our way, and started singing: "Happy Birthday to you. Happy Birthday to you, Happy Birthday, Dear Jack. Happy Birthday to you!" I was stunned! Overwhelmed! Absolutely tongue-tied!

There were my colleagues from the psych department; others from social work, biology, sociology, botany, and physics; university administrators; townspeople; all my graduate students—and many I didn't even know.

Helen led me to a table near the front where several couples of our closest friends joined us. My eyes were so filled with tears, I could see only an ocean of smiling, laughing faces. What could I say? What could I do? And that little imp, Hely was convulsing with laughter and kept hugging me. The rascal! This was all her doing. I suddenly remembered. My seventieth birthday was in two days. I hunched down in silence at the table. There was a line at the food table.

Later, I found she had contracted with the hotel, issued all the invitations including those abroad, and made each one promise secrecy; it would be her surprise. She told me afterwards she was afraid somebody would give the secret away. I wondered how much this bash had cost her. I could guess, but wouldn't dare to have asked—and she wouldn't have told me. There were no checks written on the Ours account.

There was more yet to come. After the dinner, Fred, her boss at the counseling center, took the podium, quieted the crowd, and made some remarks about me that were so flattering I was embarrassed.

He then read from a stack of letters, words of acclaim and congratulation from professors, colleagues, friends, and associates from all over the country, even several from foreign countries. In shocked silence I sat, while the crowd laughed or clapped when a specially humorous or well-written one was presented.

When Fred was finally finished, he said, "Jack, will you come up and say a few words?"

Me say a few words? I was tongue-tied, flabbergasted, and I was expected to speak. What could I say? Thank you for coming? Thank you, Helen, for arranging all this? Grasping for anything that I could say intelligently, I remembered a joke that might break the tension. I told one about the ninety-year-old, retired Supreme Court judge who was walking down a street in Miami Beach accompanied by a colleague. They accosted two beautiful, young bathing beauties dressed in bikinis. The judge paused a moment and followed them with his eyes while he exclaimed, "My! What I wouldn't give to be seventy again."

That brought the house down. I was able to mumble a few more inane comments, then return to my seat. There was a standing ovation.

The band came in with their instruments, my Dixieland band, the Town-Gown Music Appreciation Society. They played all the old familiar numbers while Helen and I danced—in a fog of ecstasy.

At midnight we threaded our way through a flood of congratulations. At home, I collapsed into bed. Never would I forget this night. And my Helyanthe turned Helen? What else could I do but love her, love her, and love her?

Helen at a scientific conference in Vienna.

Twilight and Evening Bell

Yes, I remember! Thursday, January 10, 2001, was a cold, frosty day. She was standing by the kitchen door. It was exactly eight minutes after two.

"Where you going, Darling?"

"Don't you remember, Dummerle? Told you yesterday I had an appointment with the doctor at 2:30."

Of course. I could remember everything years ago when we were first married. Now, I would forget any appointment if she didn't remind me.

Grinning, I felt good. Whenever she laughingly called me Dummerle (stupid), I knew she loved me. But somehow I didn't want her to leave today. The streets were icy, with many wrecks.

"How about driving you there, Honey Girl?"

She stuck out her chin and screwed up her face, a sign that little Hely had just come out. Hely, that charming, stubborn, little nymph, who so delighted me—as she had Grosspapa seventy-five years ago. She could be devilish at times, especially when she regressed to her childhood in Bavaria.

"I can do it by mein selbst," the puckish five-year-old announced, shaking her head.

How like her, I thought as the kitchen door slammed shut.

I looked out. There were gloomy clouds overhead. The hum of her little red Subaru backing down the driveway faded away. I would never hear her speak to me again.

The day had started as usual. Someone was tickling me, and a familiar voice whispered in my ear, "*Auf-stehen und arbeiten.*"

It was some time before I could realize what was going on. Drowsily I mused, "Do all German women rouse their spouses with a 'Get up and go to work'?"

However, the hugging I was enjoying was very warm and pleasant. I was in no hurry to get up, turn on the furnace, and feed Cleo her dollop of the good food, the kind in the can. If I didn't give her enough, she would whine, and her mistress, unable to stand her begging, would give her more—violating the veterinarian's instruction. The doctor at Cats-on-Broadway had warned us, "Cleo's much too fat. Give her mostly the dry food, or she'll get liver disease."

I retreated to our warm bed, and was in the midst of further cuddling when Cleo, having finished her breakfast, jumped on the bed and snuggled between me and my sweetheart. Helen proceeded to cradle her baby. Being temporarily replaced, I rolled over and went half-asleep again.

The sounds of singing accompanied by a splashing of water in the tub brought me alert as I heard (accompanied by laughing), "Come in and do your duty." Like a good soldier I knew my duty when the commander spoke. I opened the bathroom door.

"Close the door. You're letting the cold in."

My duty was to soap her back and scratch anywhere it itched, generally her shoulders. "Where do you want to go for breakfast today?" I queried. We often ate out at Ruby's, the Green Tree, or that Irish place with the name I couldn't remember, but which I called "Shillelagh."

"I don't feel like going out today," she replied with a note of worry in her voice.

When she didn't feel like our customary date for breakfast I would get the special coffee she so enjoyed. So, while she prepared eggs and bacon, I warmed her car, lined up at the little kiosk five blocks away, retrieved a large plastic cup of cappuccino with soy and returned home for breakfast. After coffee she'd not grump at me.

"We've got a lot of things to do today," she announced. A lot of things meant that I must get our article for the journal finished, while she went to her trainer.

It was fun teasing her about that trainer, like when I would tell our friends, "Her trainer teaches her when to sit and when to fetch." She always just laughed.

After returning from the trainer she started all the things to do. Many other people had needs: The children of our friends had birthdays coming. The gifts must be wrapped. Her group, who swam and exercised every Monday and Wednesday in the pool at The Women's Club, needed tending. She was their unofficial mother hen, lovingly taking care of everyone in that little brood of middle-aged and elderly "chicks."

"Jack, would you mind running off thirty-five copies of this list of names and addresses on the Xerox?"

Helen wouldn't be back from the doctor's for at least an hour. I had a few items I needed to buy at the Ace Hardware. So, assuring that Cleo was inside and would not be locked out on this cold, wintry day, I bundled up and proceeded to warm up my car.

On returning half an hour later, I noticed there was a light on the telephone pager. Lifting the receiver, I heard the voice of Marvin, my stepson. "Pop, I've been trying to reach you. Something terrible has happened to Mom. Meet me at the emergency room, Community Hospital."

I dashed out, squealed the car tires from the garage to the street, and floorboarded the gas pedal. Oblivious that I was far exceeding the speed limit, I growled to myself, "Don't care if I do hear a siren. Maybe the police will clear a way for me." No siren. Then, jumpy at each stoplight, I impatiently waited for it to turn green.

Double-parking at the hospital parking lot, I rushed in and was confronted by two doctors who ushered me to a single bed where she was lying immobile with her mouth partly open. "She's suffered a massive brain hemorrhage," said Dr. Nichols. Seeing my anguished face, he added, "She was happy, her usual vivacious self, and joked with the nurse. No symptoms. Then, while I was talking to her, she complained of a headache and said, 'I feel strange.' Suddenly she vomited.

"I put her in a wheelchair and had her moved immediately to Emergency. It's less than five minutes away. When she arrived there she was comatose. I've called a neurosurgeon."

Dr. Mack, the neurosurgical consultant, who was standing beside Dr. Nichols, stepped forward and said, "We've given her a thorough brain scan. I could operate, but I don't believe she would survive the surgery. There is a bare chance that we can stop the bleeding in time, but it's doubtful. Her cerebellum is flooded now, and increasingly so with every minute. If she doesn't die during the operation, she likely will in the next day or two."

Stunned, I could barely gasp, "If the surgery is successful, what will she be like afterward?"

"She will never be ambulatory again. She may live a little longer, but she will not be normal. She could be completely vegetative. You must decide now whether or not I operate."

"How long do I have to decide, Doctor?"

"Five minutes!"

Helen and I had often discussed the possibility of a crisis like this, but usually with the thought that, since I was several years older, I would probably be the one to go first. And we had both agreed on what should be done regardless of which of us it was.

"One more question, Doctor—if she were a member of your own family what would you do?"

"If it was my mother, I know that she would not want a meaningless existence preserved. In your wife's case the odds are against even that."

I knew what Helen would have wanted. I had always loved and protected her. She appreciated and often commented on the reassurance my strength gave her. It was time for courage. Sobbing uncontrollably, I could barely mutter, "Let her go!"

I remember. Yes, for many months I remember, and I am there! The hubbub has quieted. The doctors are gone. Once in a while a nurse peeps into the room. Only Marvin and I are there. Helen is lying on the bed—not a single movement. She is breathing, slowly.

Is it Marvin or somebody else who is saying to me, "Have you eaten?" Well no, I haven't, but maybe I should. At that moment a thought comes to me—one that will be with me often in the coming days. *What does she want me to do?* Of course. She will want me to eat. Marvin repeats, "Maybe you better go eat. I'll stay with her."

Helen was a good eater and a gourmet cook. When Marvin went to the Vietnam War she prepared going-away dinners for him and his friends several nights in a row. There was French night, German night, Italian night, etc., when she cooked each kind of food. She used to say, "In Bavaria, if the man isn't fat, his Frau is obviously not a good wife." Yes, Helen will want me to eat. So I will go eat.

Making my way back to the parking lot a thought occurs: *Why not just eat here at the hospital?* The idea seems revolting! How can I eat here when Helen is upstairs dying? I get in my car, drive for a while, and turn into the parking lot of a restaurant Helen and I frequented. Stopping, I sit quietly in the car for a few minutes. "No, I can't go in. She's not with me! It will not be right," I murmur to myself. Turning around, I return to the highway.

Maybe I can go someplace where I occasionally eat alone—those days when Helen doesn't want to go out. How about the 4B's? I race up Highway 93 and turn into the 4B parking lot. I sit there a moment, and get panicky. Where is Helen? No! She is back at the hospital. I will go back and eat there!

Thinking of those moments in retrospect I must have acted like the mother elephant on the animal channel whose baby has died, and who was rushing back and forth, not knowing what to do. I return to the hospital, find the restaurant, and order vegetable soup. She greatly approves of eating vegetables. *What's the matter with this soup? It has no taste! Maybe needs salt? Doesn't make it better.*

I return to the room. Marvin leaves to eat, and I am alone with the silent form of my darling. No words from her. No movement.

Years ago, when I was first married and a young experimental psychologist, I heard that sleeping people could understand what was said to them. Maybe Helen can hear me if I speak to her? "Honey, dear! Can you hear me? You know I love you, always will!" I keep this up for several minutes. No reaction from her.

Later, Helen's daughter arrives, having driven 150 miles. On seeing her mother she bursts into hysterical crying. She can cry. Helen taught me to cry, but Marvin doesn't cry. It is not manly, and he looks away.

A nurse comes in and says, "There's nothing you can do. Go home and get some rest." I go home and fall in bed, exhausted.

My eyes open slowly. They are blurred. Light seeps through the pale blue shutters. What time is it? The little clock over there looks foggy. Ten o'clock. We have an appointment downtown at eleven o'clock! I sit up, wide alert, staring at the pictures all neat, orderly, arranged by her. With hammer and nails I had tried each spot as she remarked, "Up a little. Now more to the left. That's right.

Put it there." And I would hammer the nail in the right location.

Between the two walls, directly in front of the bed, sits the TV. *Stupid thing! Why does everybody waste so much time, passively watching artificial love on the boob tube?* On the closet to my right hangs a calendar scroll for 2002. Its borders are brightly colored with young people dancing in dirndls and lederhosen (peasant costumes). The title says in old German script, "Welcome from Vienna." The bedroom is just as Helen always wanted it. Everything there in its place. Nothing missing!

It is time to say, "Good morning, Beautiful!" and get my usual hug and a kiss. I reach across the king-sized bed. Nobody is there! *Huh! She's probably out in the kitchen feeding Cleo.* Cleo must have stood outside the bedroom door waiting patiently. Obviously, Helen got up, and Cleo begged for the good food. Helen can't resist Cleo when she whines.

How come I've slept so long! I turn over toward her side of the bed. If she is awake first, she will be quietly watching me with her big eyes filled with love. She will smile and give me that kiss when I come alive.

A cloud beats down on me. *Oh yes, Helen died yesterday.* It overwhelms me with blackness. *Helen died yesterday!* A horrible pain seizes my being. Unendurable anguish! Yet it isn't a physical torment. Just an engulfing sick feeling.

Conscious awareness returns. Helen died yesterday! She died yesterday.

The torment lasts only a second or two—like when you turn on a bright light that flashes and then goes dead. I turn it off. The terrible feeling is gone, but I feel dead!

Am I really alive? I stretch out the legs. Yes, they stir, but they seem like sticks. They are made of wood, like a puppet. They move, but not by me! Somebody else is pulling the strings. The pain is gone, but I am just a frozen robot. I don't feel! Only cold logic is there.

Helen died yesterday. Yes, she died yesterday. I must get up. It's below zero today. Go warm up the car. Helen and I have an appointment downtown today. Oh yes, at the funeral home. We've got to get going.

❧

In typical German fashion, Helen always planned ahead and arranged for everything. I didn't need to. She would handle it. She took care of our business. I used to tell friends that she was my executive secretary, and that I gave her a ten percent raise every year. She would laugh and remark dryly, "Ten percent of nothing doesn't amount to much."

So we have to go to the funeral home and make the arrangements.

Ten years ago she had read a notice that advertised burial plots at the cemetery for a discount if paid immediately. The man in the gray suit showed us two plots together on the side for veterans, where I will be buried. Of course, I will die first, being older than her. It was right under a big green ash tree. We signed and paid for the plots. Helen had commented, "The shade will be nice during the summer's heat." We both laughed!

I am alone, talking to the funeral director. The funeral home was notified of her death by the hospital and has retrieved her body. It is being prepared. He does not show it to me, but takes me into a room filled with caskets. The front ones are beautiful, polished hardwood and gold embossed. They are magnificent and cost about ten thousand dollars. No! Helen doesn't want something ostentatious. She doesn't think we should spend a lot on our funerals.

At the end of the line he shows me a plain wooden box. Disgusting! Helen must have respect. I confer with her. She whispers to me, "You don't have to get one of those big expensive ones, Darling. I won't feel comfortable in it!"

We settle for one in the middle–gray, slightly blue, unassuming, but dignified. She deserves respect! Yes, my sweetheart deserves all the respect and love I can give her.

There is more business to take care of: dress, hairdo, makeup. Helen always made herself beautiful before she went out in public. That is the way she wants it now. I pore through her jewel box and find some earrings that seem to match the gorgeous party dress she bought in Singapore. She sure looked beautiful in it at the Vienna Congress. We danced to Strauss waltzes. Remembering that night, I smile!

"We need an obituary," says the director, "and a picture of her."

"Oh yes," I agree in a wooden voice. The idea courses very slowly through my foggy brain. An obituary? I will go home and write it.

I write an obituary, the high points of her life, what she will be remembered for. I rush it back to the funeral home. "We'll see that the newspaper gets a copy," reassures the director.

I leave. On the way home I think, *Today's Saturday. Maybe if I get a copy to the paper today they will print it tomorrow in the big Sunday edition! The funeral will be Wednesday. What if the funeral home forgets to turn it in to the paper until Monday or Tuesday? People won't know!*

I speed home, get another copy, and rush to the offices of *The Missoulian*. The door is locked. I bang on it! Nobody comes. I cruise around the building, looking through every window and pounding on any door I can find. Finally, somebody comes—a young woman. "Will you please put this on the desk of the editor who handles obituaries?"

"No problem," she replies, smiling. I go home and sit in silence. The obituary is published in the Sunday edition. The funeral home prints the program with her picture and the poem written on our anniversary. They provide many extra copies. Helen will be pleased!   It occurs to me I should let our closest friends know of Helen's leaving. They will be shocked. I fax copies of the funeral program, her picture, and the obituary to several of them. I will be responsible! Yes! I will be responsible—take care of things, as she would. Helen will be pleased.

The funeral is a dignified affair. Many attend, especially from the university. The funeral parlor opens up a whole reserve section of the chapel. They bring in more chairs. There isn't enough standing room.

In his usual stolid manner Helen's son, Marvin, introduces the speakers and speaks words of tribute. Jim, her longtime colleague and sparring partner, describes several humorous combats. Fred, the director at the university counseling center, talks about "the Cookie Lady." Then a tribute is read from Sascha, her grandson, who is on a modeling job in Milan. My professional robot persona delivers a talk on "The Life of Hely and Jack" in its best lecturing style—but I am not really present.

Norm Taylor, concert pianist (and university graduate dean), plays beautiful music, providing a moment for prayers and memories. We all cry to ourselves, quietly. Helen approves!

Afterwards, the ladies of her swimming group—Recycled Teens—provide light refreshments. Many people, many handshakes, many hugs, many tears are shared.

I look the other way when they close the casket. She isn't there, my darling, even though that figure wears her prettiest dress! It doesn't smile. Helen always smiled and laughed. She must be around somewhere, but not in that gray box!

At the cemetery, they bring the coffin with the flowers on it. They place it over a hole, dug with difficulty in the frozen ground. I stand beside it and speak some words of affection, "Honey Girl! I'll always love you!"

I know she is not really in that casket. She is in the wind! She is in the big ash tree! She is in the clouds, the mountains and streams of Montana. And she is with me—in my heart!

On a Caribbean cruise.

THE SECRET HEART
OF A WOMAN

It is rarely that a man is granted access to the secret heart of a woman—and especially his spouse, while she is alive or afterwards. And it is in the nature of a woman to pride herself on being a mystery to her man, one that he will never completely solve.

However, there are many things about their spouses that women tell other women. Not necessarily good, nor necessarily bad. Just personal (men wouldn't understand.). In seeking material for writing this book about Helyanthe's personhood, I was told many things by some of her women friends—by those companions in her swimming class at the Women's Club who wrote long letters of condolence; by Peg, a school counselor and long-term buddy of Helen's; or by Julie, the sparkling lady who cleaned our teeth at the dentist four times a year.

Our one-hour appointments for teeth cleaning were always adjacent to one another. Sometimes I went first; sometimes Helen. If Helen was first, I knew she would have talked about me, I found in quite complimentary terms.

> Julie: Your wife told me a lot of things you've
> been doing.
> Jack (facetiously): Don't believe a word of it. I
> wasn't even there.
> Julie (laughing): Oh, they were flattering.

What she said was often music to my ears. Sometimes she told me real gems. Other times, I recognized Helen used Julie as a way of sending me messages indirectly.

"Huh. She probably told you how absentminded I am these days."

If I was first, I usually told Julie imaginary offenses that I knew were not true. They could be counted on to stall off the moment when Julie would start unpleasantly digging into my gums, which I had neglected. It was a fun game.

From such sources I learned that Helen considered me the perfect husband, a very confusing revelation, since I didn't think of myself as such, knew I wasn't, and had experienced a very, very different picture of myself from two previous wives. But after I had written all the foregoing in this book, I was to learn even more about Helen's inner views. Exploring the cupboards, drawers, and closets a year after her death, I found where she hid her secret heart, where she bared her very soul.

Back in the farthest dark corner of her clothes closet lay a portable iron file case filled with old papers. It was almost totally concealed by piles of income tax folders, books on cooking, newspapers, and magazines. What was in that iron box? What secrets would come to light? I could barely control my excitement.

One glance into its contents revealed it brimming with personal material. There were all the love letters I had ever written her, poems, valentines, notes, mementos, and diary-type messages written by her to herself. There were also many letters from other people, most of whom I did not know. Although curious, I recognized these as sacred ground. Dare I thrust my clumsy hands into this confidential treasury of my sweetheart?

At that time, I was too overcome with personal sorrow. Besides, I had great quantities of memories of friends, family, clients, and my own, plus travel records and correspondence with colleagues and publishers. It would take me a long time to sort these out and write them up in the book chapters being organized.

Later, when I had recovered some emotional stability I thought I could handle it—not recognizing that more floods of tears would be released. Locking the door, and reclining in my easy chair, I spilled the contents of that box onto a large table. *What are you going to tell me, Sweetheart—about yourself, and about us?*

It soon became clear that I must organize this enormous quantity of materials. So I sorted them into piles: newspaper clippings, holiday cards (Christmas, Valentine's Day, birthdays, and "un-birthdays"), poems, books of poems, travel records, workshops, and other scientific presentations, plus letters to her from other people. These were her *inner* personhood.

As I sorted the materials out, especially the last, a sober mood replaced my little-boy curiosity. It had an ethical, religious quality. What business had I here? Dare I delve into her very private soul? All this material was not saved for me, never intended for my eyes. Like her personal therapy notes on clients, they were confidential to her. Perhaps I should destroy all this material immediately. As I have so often done since she left, I relaxed and asked her, "Beautiful, what shall I do with all this material you saved? What would you want me to do?"

As usual, an answer returned, but whether it really came from her, or was only a product of my own curiosity and imagination I will never know: "Do what you think right, Darling. I trust you completely." So I started with those items about which there could be no question, the newspaper clippings.

They were mostly about me, not her. Every letter to the editor I had sent to *The Missoulian*, every notice of a university promotion, a special lecture I gave somewhere, an award I received, or an opinion of mine published—much of which I had completely forgotten. My God, everything for over thirty years! Why did she save in this, her inner heart, every item of my activities? Momentarily, I had a tinge of regret and recognized my own self-centeredness. In fact, I felt sad, ashamed. I had not saved those of hers. Did I love her less than she loved me? Or was I merely an unthinking male?

Next, the holiday cards, often inscribed with long poems or other messages of love: years of valentines, anniversaries, Christmases, birthdays, and the un-birthday cards we sent occasionally—so as to remind each other of our love when it was not expected. Some of the poems were not bad. Some were terrible.

Then there were the letters. During the early years of our marriage we were often apart. Each of us had travel obligations. She gave workshops throughout Montana and traveled abroad with her daughter or son. I gave courses at other universities: UCLA, the University of Oregon, the State University of New York at Binghamton, and a college in Switzerland. She also included documentation of the editing of a film on multiple personalities in Los Angeles, plus many papers from scientific congresses in foreign lands.

I never realized the reams of love letters I had written in those days, sharing places and events, but mostly about how I missed her. She never seemed to tire of them. Why didn't I save hers too? She wrote back almost every day, and I had waited for the post like a starving child.

Digging deeper, I began to learn more new things about Helen. She wrote a letter to our best friend, a psychologist, known affectionately as "Fig," in which she described her various ego states. They were depicted as follows:

> Let me introduce my selves as I, the observer, see them. It will be a new experience. I wonder what I will write.

> *The Professional*: She, an intellectual, is respected at the university, goes to professional meetings, and tunes in well to her patients.

The Lady: She is charming and uses her listening skills to oil social conversation, but is not truly involved. I find her dull and phony.

The Teenager: A powerful force, she is my problem child. Brash, lots of fun, exhibitionistic, and doesn't give a damn what anybody thinks. Totally real and authentic, but she gets me into trouble sometimes. Loves to fight for fun, to throw out insults, and tends to come out with men. Likes alcohol but never gets drunk. She feels around nineteen, and with her energy can raise havoc with a body that's past fifty. She has guts, is unafraid, and will try anything. Likes to shock the prudish, staid, and dull people.

The Ten-Year-Old: A younger version of the Teenager, frisky, giddy, harmless, fun. She comes out with Jack, who finds her amusing. I won't let her out in the world. Jack refers to both the Teenager and Ten-Year Old as "Hely." He likes them because they make him feel young.

The Opera Star: Unfortunately, she can't sing. She comes out in teaching, needs to show off. Is out when Jack and I do workshops together. Our teaching workshops are never dull. She adds the excitement, but couldn't do them without Jack. He is the intellectual heavyweight.

Then me, the *Mother* ego state who is writing. I've never clarified myself to me so well before.

In another letter to her son, written a year before we began our relationship, I was to receive much new information about her early idealism. I remember she had already showed it to me years ago, so I didn't feel any breach of confidence in reading it again now.

It was ten pages, single spaced, and headed "This I Believe," in which she outlined her philosophy of life at that time under such topics as: sex, education, patriotism, religion, books, joy, beauty, humor, idealism, romanticism, prayer, work, balance, drugs, drinking, hippies and rebellion, and responsibility.

Was she different then from when I knew her? Not really, but several of the items surprised me.

> *Patriotism*: I feel good about the United States. It has offered an opportunity that I could never have had in Germany.
>
> I believe in the democracy we have. I get choked up in a Fourth of July parade, as well as when the flag passes by. I owe my adopted country allegiance and faith; yet I am also grateful for my German heritage. It has given me pride in good workmanship. My Bavarian background, how to relax in play in the form of convivial camaraderie or *Gemütlichkeit*.*

Religion and Prayer: She was then an active churchgoing, Lutheran Sunday-school teacher. Later she moved away from Christian views of heaven and hell, and miracles into a Unitarian-Universalist concept of God, whom she saw everywhere as a creative, controlling energy in the universe, perhaps like the sun, rather than as a father figure. Was she, Helyanthe, really a daughter of the sun?

---

*Good-natured cheerfulness.

Sex: After presenting the traditional views of good sex and bad sex, she then gives some startling ones, perhaps Victorian, but not in accord with accepted, contemporary beliefs.

> In sex, as in other male-female relationships, I believe in the double standard. Premarital sex is good for the gander, but not for the goose. But when a fellow can get a girl without marrying her, he loses respect for her, and he certainly doesn't want a wife he can't respect.

So she advocates sex for young men with girls they don't intend to marry! Wow! What a blow to current views of equality. Does it come from her European background? I never realized until now how important this concept was in her belief system.

I knew that occasionally, when treating a college boy with sexual problems, she would advise him to go to the mining town of Wallace, the nearby Idaho sin town. The many notorious girlie houses, established to keep the miners happy, had existed there for a hundred years.

In her own male relationships she was a Victorian. She loved many close friends, but was herself not physically intimate with them. And that's the way she kept me until we had committed to each other.

❦

Some of the letters revealed there were other men before me who wanted to marry her. Why wouldn't other men desire such a wonderful lady as their wife? Apparently they weren't just right for her. She affectionately and sensitively sent them away—without damaged egos. Their letters were not meant for me to see. Respect was deserved by everyone—her, them, and me. So I decided not to read them, but to treat them as her personal, intimate property—and simply shred them. They were a part of her inner heart, and belonged to her.

There was one very intimate problem that confronted her. I did not realize its magnitude then. At the time I fell in love with her, I had already moved out of my previous household, had initiated divorce proceedings, and had provided for my wife's financial security and for our little ones still with her. I had moved (unhappily) to a small rented room.

My father, a man greatly respected in his community, had installed in me a strong sense of duty: "If you give your word, Son, you keep it, no matter how inconvenient or painful." I had given my word to my ex-wife. She had spent twenty-five years with me caring for our household and mothering our four children. I could not simply abandon her to fend for herself. We had agreed on terms of the divorce (which I insisted on) that allocated a substantial part of my income so she and the child still at home could live in comfort and dignity.

Was that enough? Had I fulfilled my obligations? She had shared my hearth, though for many years not my heart. We had grown apart. Marital counseling had been unsuccessful. It was not healthy for both of us to continue an artificial relationship. But Helen wasn't sure. She was suffering great anguish, the deepest conflict within herself, which she didn't betray to me. Not that I didn't love her as well as any man could love, or that once free I would not marry her, but that I might stay with her for the wrong reasons.

She put it in a many-paged letter that shocked me to the core of my being. It gave me for the first time a comprehension of our relationship that I would never have thought of. Here, I dare give only a few of its most telling sentences. It was like Hamlet's soliloquy and was addressed to "Dear Helyanthe," (from the realist to the romanticist) as follows:

> I want to caution you not to do anything by
> behaving in such a way that would be con-
> trary to the basic values of you that are at

the core of you. [She was talking about whether or not to go to bed with me, but not for the reasons I, a man, would have thought.]

You say you love this man. I really believe that. I don't question that this is the man of your dreams, the kind of man you hoped for in a husband. Now he has form, substance; he lives, he breathes. Yes, listen—as miserable as you are, think of how lucky you are. Very few human beings ever experience this depth of feeling for another human being. It has a godlike quality, spiritual, ethereal, intangible. The only way to believe it is to experience it. You love him; so do I. We are agreed on this point. Now what?

Men are generally quicker to come to a passionate response than women; for this reason it is easier for the woman to curb the behavior, and also her responsibility to do so. When you don't curb this behavior, you put him in a very frustrating situation, and that really isn't very loving behavior on your part. You know there are names for women who do this sort of thing. OK. I know this idea hurts. Take your head out of the sand. You are being doubly unfair to him, because this man finds security in control. This is an age-old game between the male and the female.

You are closer to consummating this relationship than you think. What about those lingerie sales at the mercantile? Why do you need three negligees, a peignoir, and silk slippers? Who do you think you're kid-

ding? I'm just trying to get you to face what
you're doing.

Another thing. What does this man
think of you? How does he feel about you?
He is a human being with feet of clay, even
if he does seem superhuman to your befud-
dled, irrational, non compos mentis mind.
Does he love you?

He doesn't intentionally hurt anyone
(not consciously anyway). Never involves
himself totally in a relationship; never
invests his whole self, so he doesn't get hurt.
His modus operandi in living is much more
sensible than yours. Of course, he misses the
Olympian heights of joy, but he misses the
pangs of hell, too. It is this control, this
strength in him that appeals to you.

Now what are the alternatives? Either
consummate the relationship or break it off.
There is no in-between for you. This man is
your nemesis. In other male relationships in
the past you have been a master of keeping
them from becoming too warm and at the
same time still being involved. It must be
the counselor in you. Now, you don't just
feel like the counselor toward this man, do
you? You have never learned to be someone
other than you are. You remind me of the
expression in "Rowan & Martin's Laugh-
In": "My God, Goldie, but you're dumb!"
The only reason I tolerate you is because you
are obviously an integral part of me.

During this period Helen was acting like a marital counselor to me, constantly probing how I felt toward my wife,
and, if anything, pressuring me to seek a reconciliation with
her.

So it's either yes or no. Suppose you say no.
What will life be like? Miserable, lonely for
certain. You loved your first husband, but at
the age of twenty neither of you were capable of the depth of feeling now possible.

Suppose you say yes; what will he
expect? A relationship that is warm and loving at the moment, but one that makes no
demands? He wants no problems with a
wife, so that means the relationship will be
cautious.

Since I had stayed so many years in an unhappy marriage
out of a sense of duty, Helen feared that, even if I married
(and especially if she had an affair with me) I might be doing
so out of a sense of duty. Or that after romance and passion
had faded, I might stay with her out of a sense of responsibility, and our marriage would become a prison to me. That she
could not do to me. It would not be loving behavior on her
part. She loved me so much, she was prepared to give me up.

Now what would the relationship seem to
you, and how would you respond? To you,
this man is the beginning and the end, the
alpha and omega of your existence. You are
not sophisticated. All you know is total
involvement, total commitment, total
love—the rosy glow of flickering candlelight
that distorts reality.

This kind of total commitment is you
because you are not a femme fatale; you are
just a *Hausfrau*—a one-man woman—that's
all. You would be completely faithful to him,
and he would end up being miserable. You
simply can't do that to him—not if you really love him. Let him go; let him find another.

Then she types with different margins the following:

Oh, my God, give me strength; I do love him.
I do. Give me the strength to say good-bye.
PLEASE, PLEASE, PLEASE.

Jack Watkins in the Army, World War II.

THE ROMANTIC HEART OF A MAN

This chapter wasn't supposed to have been written. It changes the whole thrust of the book—and its ending. But because of the revelations I found in Helyanthe's secret heart it has been forced on me.

This book was to be a tribute to her, a story of her personhood, her essence, her healing gift, her humanity. My role was to be only that of an observer, with perhaps some interaction as her husband and constant companion. Now, because of what she revealed in her secret file, I must write this chapter to bring closure; with a realization of the enormity of what I found in her treasure chest, I have been dragged onstage in a major role. If I don't also reveal the "Heart of a Man," the story will be incomplete.

As I lay for two hours in bed weeping this morning, I realized that you can't write a love story and tell only half of what happened. I am forced to relate the rest as I experienced it.

At the end of her self-written "Letter from Realist to Romanticist," Helen begged for the strength to say goodbye to me. She found it. I was not aware then she was in an emotional crisis, waging an internal battle with herself, one that could mean happiness or pain to both of us. How dumb men can be! But shortly thereafter, I had received a four-page letter as follows:

> My dearest love! It is now one hour after you left, and I've been sitting, thinking, digesting all we had both said to each other this afternoon. I believe I understand you more. I also love you more.
>
> Your actual words said something like this: "I'm afraid I'm going to hurt you. I can't measure up to the love you feel for me."

She then turns to her third ear and believes that her unconscious translates as follows:

> Your love is a threat and a burden to me that is going to make me feel guilty. My wife isn't that bad. I should stop the divorce proceedings and try to straighten out my marriage. I don't want to have an affair with you. This is wrong. I care what happens to you.

She continues:

> My seeming pure and holy love for you made you feel guilty? Oh, what a sham! How horrible of me, Hans! You would hate me for that. How terrible, how frightening to me!
>
> Could you marry a woman with whom you had an affair? You are a man of integrity, of honor, of love, and of real humanness.
>
> Our continued relationship is not good for either of us.

She then speaks of my "resentment and hostility toward women," and wonders if "some of the resentments you express toward your wife belong to your first wife or toward your mother?"

She then asks:

> If after your divorce you married me (even though that is what I most want), how do you think I would feel? I would always feel

partially, if not wholly, responsible. And the
rest of my life, to expiate my sin, you'd be
married to a martyr. How awful! How sick! I
need your respect.

Goodbye! Don't feel badly. Knowing
you has been the most beautiful, the most
rewarding experience I have ever known. I
shall be eternally grateful. (I know this is the
right decision for I feel quiet inside.)

Ich liebe dich!

Helyanthe

This was but a fraction of what she wrote, but it is the
crucial part. She adds a note: "Please return these pages in
person. I want to say goodbye to you in person, at home."

My first reaction? Shock! She says she loves me pro-
foundly, passionately; how could she say "Goodbye?" But she
was decisive, so positive. What is wrong with me?

I knew women can leave you when they no longer love
you; I had experienced that. But Hely was leaving me
because she loved me very much—maybe too much. To a
man this made no sense.

I studied her every word. Maybe she didn't really mean
it. You know how women are! They often change their
minds. As Virgil wrote: *Varium et mutabile simper Femina.**
Man-thinking. Huh? Could she really mean it?

Shortly after, in a phone call she informed me that she
had decided to make a trip back to Bavaria, visit her relatives, and "maybe decide whether she was really an
American or a German." That last hint sounded ominous.
Perhaps she wouldn't come back from Germany! After all,
her loved brother/uncle, physician, Siegfried, was in
Munich. Nonsense! She loved being an American citizen,
and she truly loved me. As her husband, I could make her
very happy. We would have a wonderful life together. But
the more I thought the more I became concerned.

---

*A fickle and changeable thing is woman ever.

Among the traits she inferred I had was a resentment
toward women, but a very strong sense of duty—to protect
them and her. She also worried that perhaps I could not take
her total, unconditional love, that I did not make such total
commitments in a relationship, and that in time, I would
regard our marriage as a prison—and feel miserable. Maybe
it would end as my second marriage had. Was she right in her
psychological analysis?

The sun is the source of our life and warmth. But unpro-
tected from its direct rays you can get a painful sunburn. And
if you get too close to it you can be destroyed. Was the love
of Helyanthe, my sun goddess, too hot for me to handle? Did
she think that, like Icarus, I would be destroyed if I was too
close to her? I was confused and badly worried.

Now comes what I didn't want to talk about—my own
childhood and earlier history. I know though it is relevant,
maybe crucial.

My father and mother were married in their late thirties.
Father was the epitome of responsibility—and he transmitted a strict sense of duty to me. To me, he was a god and my
model of manhood. My mother's mother died when she was
a tiny infant. Her father died when she was four, and she was
reared by two older sisters. Mother hadn't been loved, and
she never learned to love.

My parents got along well in a working partnership. But
I never saw them hug or kiss. And I don't remember ever
being cuddled by her or sitting on her lap. She was not cruel
or unkind, and took good care of me. She was a very efficient
teacher and county superintendent of schools. Was I angry
and resentful toward her? Helen was probably right; I also
didn't know how to love.

I thought about my two former wives, one of whom left
me when I was at war, and the other who gradually lost her
affection for me. Was it my lack of loving? I had obviously
adopted the role of martyr. I was passively hostile. Maybe
they weren't as much to blame for the breakups of our mar-
riages as I had thought, and Helen didn't want to be tied to

a passively hostile, unable-to-really-love husband. Must I change if I were not to lose her?

And how would she do it? I knew. She would not damage my male ego. She would write letters from Bavaria, but fewer and fewer as the weeks stretched into months, and perhaps years. She would wait for my ardor (and hers) to cool. Maybe I would get so lonely I would find somebody else and marry them. She might never stop loving me, then months or years later she could return to her beloved America and spend the rest of her life counseling college students. What would our lives be like?

No Hely and Hans. No workshops. No jointly exploring hypnosis and ego-state therapy. No traveling over the world.

And never would this book have been written.

It ought not to be that way. It should not be. *It will not be*. This crisis called for some powerful courting. No little bouquet of flowers and a goodbye kiss when I loaded her on the plane would do. That might be my last kiss from her.

What might bring her back to me? I know. She likes my poems. I will write a book of poems to her. So about a month before she was scheduled to leave I set to writing a book of poems.

Buried among all the mementos in her secret heart I had discovered that book of poems and the letter of proposal that accompanied it. Did I write them? They read too beautifully. They're too artistic. I'm a scientist, a professor; I couldn't have written that book.

The book was seven inches square. The front cover (lavender) was a picture of the ocean at sunset—she would be going across the ocean—with the message: "Tonight, wherever you are my thoughts are of you."

The pages were in a light green, perfectly typed. In those days we had no computers; an error meant retyping the page.

What follows is the preface to the book of poems.

> At four o'clock in the morning it is dark and
> sometimes very lonely. What does one do

when faced with loss of a loved one? She should know the caliber of the man who waits for her. And if he measures not up to her needs, they both should know the reason why. And if she elects to join him in life's voyage she should never feel cheated.

My heart, my soul must speak to her. It shall be a symphony, a music of words. It speaks of hopes and fears, of love and passion, anger, doubt and ecstasy.

This work is published in one edition with a circulation of one copy. It is written for one reader who is very special and represents one-half of the human race. It will then have been read by every one who matters.

Hans

Here is my proposal letter:

July 19, 1971

To My Dearest Sweetheart, Mein Leibling, My Helyanthe:

You, who are from the sun, have brought the light into my life. I should be very proud to have you ever by my side for as long as God shall grant us life.

Today, My Darling, is your birthday. It was on a day like this that heaven smiled on your lovely mother, and she brought forth the wonderful daughter you are. I have thought much as to what might be presented for an appropriate recognition on this festive occasion. These flowers are for you, but they are offered in memory of, and as a tribute to her, who created this sunshine which so gladdens my world. I hope that wherever she is she will understand and smile.

As for you, My Dear, I can only offer as a gift all that I have, my love, my self, my heart and my hand—all that I am—all that I will ever be. I hope that you will choose to become my constant companion, my gracious lady, my wife. If you join me in this life's adventure we shall laugh and play and fight and love together.

Soon, great birds will carry you to the beautiful home of your childhood. There you will once again see your loved ones and rediscover the delights of that fabulous land. Enjoy it, Liebling, savoring this experience to the last drop as with rare old wine.

I am most mindful of your needs for freedom and independence, and your reservations about commitment. But Darling, if we do indeed love each other, let us not stand forever only on the threshold of a great adventure together, for:

The Bird of Time has but a little Way
To flutter—and the Bird is on the wing.[1]

The happy couple.

A Legacy of Gifts

We commonly present gifts to others to show our love for them. Helen's entire life consisted of gifts. As a baby she brought the gift of new hope to a family devastated by the aftermath of war, and the loss of a loved one. Through Helyanthe's sunshine, happiness returned to Grossvater and the others.

Overcoming many struggles and personal loss, she undertook a career of giving. By painstakingly fashioning and giving German cookies to her colleagues, she gave them symbols of her love, her culture, and herself. Her gifts then matured into the bits of psychological wisdom that saved the careers and even the lives of many students.

She didn't exist to impress others, nor to receive from others. She gave with no thought of expecting back. But it is in the nature of humans to give to those from whom we have received. Therefore, she received in abundance that which she dispensed.

Her gifts were so varied and numerous that it is difficult to apportion their relative significance. Perhaps one stands foremost, because it is the simplest for every person to give.

The Gift of Respect

Everyone seeks respect, yearns for it, and is grateful when it is received. Yet so often it is lacking. One should give respect to others, not because of their wealth, fame, or achievements, but because every bit of life in this world deserves respect—for just existing.

Having respect, we are freed from the need to compete, to challenge, and to strive for it. Helen never saw the world as a struggle between good and evil, between angels and devils. She saw it as a problem between respect and disrespect. And those to whom we attribute malevolence may be souls struggling for respect that in their youth was denied. Who knows how many Hitlers, Stalins, or Saddam Husseins would ever have developed if in their infancy they had felt completely respected and loved?

This was the philosophy in which Helen treated, laughed, and offered her gifts. No man was so evil that he could never be changed and rehabilitated.

That did not mean she was unable to hate. She could hate those who mistreated others, who in their blind race for money, power, or fame ignored the needs of others—and stamped on them.

But she could rise above that hate. If patients were loaded with hatred, she was ready to use her gift of understanding and vanquish their hates.

Many times in her therapy she unearthed hidden hatred and induced its possessor to release it in a paroxysm of rage (called abreaction). Then she would replace it with at least respect, sometimes even love. Many of her patients, through the gifts they received from Helen, were able themselves to rise above the hatreds engendered by abuse in their childhood, and join the ranks of healers, dispensing to other patients the gifts they themselves had just received.

The Gift of Laughter

We all enjoy laughter. Millions are spent on TV, movies, and books for inducing laughter. Laughter has been proven good for one's physical health. Unfortunately, some people are frozen in a cast of anger and fear. They are unable to laugh. They plod their way through life in a gray existence. Then others give not to them what they desperately seek:

attention, respect, and love. They are avoided. Sometimes their inner rage or loneliness breaks through. They take violent action against those they perceive as tormentors—and we wonder why.

Laughter is also the best antidote against the humiliation of being confronted with one's own inadequacies. Helen taught people how to face personal mistakes and admit them with self-directed laughter. Then others laugh with you, not at you.

From childhood, Helen learned the self-enhancing effects of humor. She laughed, and laughed, and laughed, sometimes at herself, and sometimes at others, but never to put others down. Often she was called upon to heal the wounds of those who had been laughed at, and whose egos were not able to take such demeaning. She helped them build the strength to deflect the taunts of others.

After her death, when all the letters of condolence and respect were received, that characteristic most repeated might be phrased: "Laughter, thy name is Helen."

The Gift of Tears

Men don't cry, or so my father taught, even as he struggled to hold back the tears at my mother's funeral. So many of us, especially we men, are afraid to pour forth our feelings of loss when a loved one has left us. This is also true when we have lost a loved pet—even a valued article, or a human cause to which we have committed ourselves.

Helen taught me to accept the gift of tears and transmit it to others. I learned that it is not a matter of shame or self-belittlement to let the tears come, relieving our burdens and pains. I had to rediscover this truth again when losing Hely.

It is false modesty that impels fathers to instruct their sons, "Men don't cry. Be a brave little man and don't cry." Thus many men remain bottled up, never true to their own selves. They present to the world an artificial pose of bravery. Helen taught that brave men can cry.

Sometimes though, they had first to master fear, then release rage, before they could accept the gift of tears. As such is the human psyche often layered.

The Gift of Understanding

You cannot hate a person you really understand. That doesn't mean you approve of their behavior, but when you understand the motives for their behavior, compassion (and sorrow) often replaces hate.

Helen was well aware of this when in the little book, Springs of Persian Wisdom, she facetiously commented, "It is hard if not impossible to hate someone you really get to know and understand. That is why I stay away from people I want to dislike."

Many years ago, in a Veterans Administration clinic, I accepted for treatment a man in his thirties who was rejected by everyone else on the staff. The general reaction was, "He shouldn't receive therapy; he should be hung." Nor could I blame anyone who felt that way.

He would come home from work each day and, wielding a large club, would beat his twelve-year-old son unmercifully—for minor, imagined transgressions. It was with great difficulty that I could stand even to listen to him. But I knew this cruelty must come from somewhere. So I said to him, "Bill, you must have been badly treated when you were a boy to have to beat your son this way!"

He burst into tears and, midst violent sobbing, told me that his father was a burglar and used to beat him every day. At that time he had vowed to himself: "There's only two kinds of people in the world, them what gives the beatings, and them what gets the beatings. When I grow up I ain't going to be them what gets the beatings."

So now we know why he is cruel to his son. By being the beater he avoids being the beaten one. He beats his son because he is still afraid of his father. He must re-experience that fear, confront it, release it, and master it.

I understood that if I told him, "You've got to stop beating your son, Bill," he would not stop. He would simply stop coming for therapy, because I would just be another rejecting, non-understanding father figure. He might even come to fear me.

We undertook a series of abreactive sessions, when he could first confront his fear, then in rage confront the image of his father. But it was difficult and painful for the next several months, while I tried to show him, by example, that there could be people in the world who were neither "them what gives the beatings" nor "them what gets the beatings."

After some three months of accepting, releasing, and noncondemning sessions, he reached self-understanding and ceased beating his son.

Helen developed this technique with great skill, and used it often in treating woman patients who had been raped in childhood.[1]

The Gift of Healing

When the storm clouds have been brushed away, when the torrents of sadness and rejection stop, when one has learned how to accept, respect, cry, and laugh, then the gift of healing becomes possible.

People often enter the health professions to meet personal needs. Adolescent confusion can motivate youths to seek answers in psychology or medicine. A physician being treated for depression recounted how he came home after school one day and was scolded by his father. Begrudgingly he went upstairs to his room, angrily muttering, "Drop dead!"

Ten minutes later his depressed father went to the basement and shot himself. The devastated lad could do nothing as he watched his father's existence bleed away. So he became a physician. Now, he was spending the rest of his life trying to rescue his father, thus to relieve his guilt.

When working with health professionals, Helen always sought a helping ego state. She assumed that, if they were therapists, they already had one within, or they would not have embarked on a healing occupation. She would activate that ego state and urge it to contribute more actively to the patient. Sometimes it was induced to take the role of an inner doctor, healing the harmful aspects of the patient's own being.

Many are the letters from therapists, physicians, psychologists, and other health professionals thanking her for rescuing their own selves and increasing their therapeutic success with others.

The Gift of Peace

Psychotherapy is an interaction between patient and therapist that aims at resolving conflicts between different parts of one's self and improving one's interactions with other people. When it is successful, one tends to feel an inner peace. The turmoil, the struggle, the frustrations are either eliminated or so lessened that they can be ignored. One finds meaning in the challenges of everyday life.

Medical practice can save a life; psychotherapy can improve its quality, bringing peace and happiness. Helen was a happy lady, and so loaded with this gift that she had an excess to bestow on others. That is why she became a role model to so many women.

She demonstrated for them that it is possible to have romance, love, children, idealism, meaning, satisfaction, pride in oneself as a woman, a successful career, and even international acclaim. No wonder many of her women friends almost worshipped her.

But she never thought of herself as a role model, nor did she promote it. It came unsought as a by-product of just being herself.

In *The Therapeutic Self*, which was dedicated to her, there is a saying attributed to that wise old psychoanalyst Wilhelm Stekel, who is reputed to have looked up from his deathbed, as if to grasp the meaning of the hundreds of lives which he had treated and, just before dying, whispered, "It's all a matter of love."

This was Helyanthe's final and ultimate gift to the world.

The Gift of Love

She loved her childhood home in Bavaria; she loved her mother, Grossvater, and her brothers. She loved her uncle and aunt in Pittsburgh; she loved her first husband, Bob, and she loved her children. She loved school and learning. She loved counseling, teaching, and treating. She loved her clients, the students in the university, plus her older patients, the health professionals who sought her grace and wisdom. She loved almost every human being she met. She loved the river of life in all its tributaries—and she loved me.

Thirty years ago, when Helyanthe came to be my bride, she brought a gift of great prophetic vision. Within the pages of that little book, *Springs of Persian Wisdom*, there is an inscription, which she wrote:

> Some day we will part—in death. So must it be. But all that we have been in life will live on in the quality of other lives that we have touched significantly. Thus we shall be reborn again and again. And in this way we are woven into the fabric of time.

On a sloping, verdant hillside, which faces the towering Montana mountains across the nestling valley, there is a large ash tree. Under that tree where she sleeps, there is a simple plate on which is engraved:

HELEN HUTH WATKINS
Helyanthe
Born July 19, 1921. Died Jan. 11, 2002
She spent her life helping others

And beside her under that same tree, there is a vacant place.

Jack and Helen in their last photograph together.

ENDNOTES

Preface
1. Watkins, J., and Watkins, H. *Ego States: Theory and Therapy*. New York: Norton, 1997.

The Cookie Lady
1. These were simple cases, requiring only brief interventions for their solution. During the following years, Helen would develop from a counselor into a sophisticated psychotherapist, using complex hypnoanalytic procedures and achieving amazing results that seemed almost miraculous.

The Secret of Miracles
1. Ego states are segments of one's personality that are normally unconscious, but which we sometimes experience like different moods. At times, they can cause us to behave as if we were different personalities. But they are not necessarily pathological, as are the states in a multiple personality disorder, which is a true mental illness. Although they are normally unconscious-meaning we are not aware of them-they can be activated and made conscious through hypnosis. Usually these segments were separated off by early traumatic experiences during childhood, or by internalizing our perceptions of some important person in our lives, such as our parents.
2. Steckler, J. Ego state therapy: A workshop—with John and Helen Watkins. *Trauma and Recovery*, October 1989, pp. 25–26.
3. Watkins, J.G. *The Therapeutic Self*. New York: Human Sciences Press, 1978.
4. Watkins, J.G. *General Psychotherapy*. Third edition. Springfield: Charles Thomas, 1960.

Dare the Impossible

1. Watkins, J.G. Hypnotic hypermnesia and forensic hypnosis: A cross-examination. *American Journal of Clinical Hypnosis*, 32: 71–83, 1989.
2. Helen published this procedure: Watkins, H.H. Treating the trauma of abortion. *Pre- and Peri-natal Psychology*. Winter: 135–142, 1986.
3. An obstetrician who read the report of this case stated that when a fetus is threatened, it often retreats back into the uterine wall to protect itself.
4. Theoretical note: In the chapter "The Secret of Miracles," the psychological process of resonance was explained, in which Helen would take the representation of her patient (the total of all her perceptions of him—visual, auditory, tactile, etc.) and by infusing this internal object with her self energy, be for the moment the other person. Helen could then personally experience the other's internal world as if it were her own.

Here she does the reverse. She hypnotically isolates a part of the self of her patient, one that came from Amy's identifying with the destructive feelings of her parents. By focusing and interpretation (within a hypnotic regression) she removes Amy's self energy from that internal, destructive ego state (Monster, Angel of Death). This turns it back from self into an object. It becomes now only the memory of a perception, which the patient can expunge from herself. Amy will no longer feel an inner voice telling her to kill herself. She can lose her depression— one that seems to have existed since she was "a dot."

The Romantic Heart of a Man

1. From *The Rubaiyat of Omar Khayyam*.

A Legacy of Gifts

1. Watkins, J.G., and Watkins, H.H. The psychodynamics and initiation of effective abreactive experiences. *Hypnos*, XXVII: 60–67, 2000.

About the Author

John G. Watkins PhD, Professor Emeritus of the University of Montana, is world renowned as a pioneering psychologist, particularly in the areas of hypnosis, dissociation, and multiple personality. He was a founder and past president of ISCEH, an international society in hypnosis. He has been the president of the Society for Clinical and Experimental Hypnosis (SCEH), of the American Board of Psychological Hypnosis, and of the Hypnosis Division of the American Psychological Association. Dr. Watkins has also served as clinical editor of the *International Journal of Clinical and Experimental Hypnosis*. He has lectured all over the world and authored many groundbreaking books and articles on hypnosis and psychotherapy, making him one of the leading theorists in the field.

Dr. Watkins received his Bachelor's Degree and Master's Degree from University of Idaho and his Ph.D. from Columbia University. He went on to teach at University of Montana, Auburn University, and Washington State University. He served as chief psychologist at Portland, Oregon's Veterans Administration Hospital and the Chicago Veterans Hospital. He has received many awards and has been interviewed on national TV by William Buckley (PBS), Morley Safer (*60 Minutes*), and Geraldo. One of his best-known successes was to get the notorious Hillside Strangler to confess to murder and to reveal his multiple personalities. John Watkins lives near Denver, Colorado.

Sentient Publications, LLC publishes books on cultural creativity, experimental education, transformative spirituality, holistic health, new science, and ecology, approached from an integral viewpoint. Our authors are intensely interested in exploring the nature of life from fresh perspectives, addressing life's great questions, and fostering the full expression of the human potential. Sentient Publications' books arise from the spirit of inquiry and the richness of the inherent dialogue between writer and reader.

We are very interested in hearing from our readers. To direct suggestions or comments to us, or to be added to our mailing list, please contact:

SENTIENT PUBLICATIONS, LLC
1113 Spruce Street
Boulder, CO 80302
303.443.2188
contact@sentientpublications.com
www.sentientpublications.com